Tragedy & Trust

*Can You Still Trust God
After Losing a Child?*

Thom Vines with
John Michael Vestal

authorHOUSE®

AuthorHouse™
1663 Liberty Drive
Bloomington, IN 47403
www.authorhouse.com
Phone: 1-800-839-8640

First published by AuthorHouse 2/16/2011

ISBN: 978-1-4567-2789-5 (dj)
ISBN: 978-1-4567-2790-1 (e)
ISBN: 978-1-4567-2791-8 (sc)

Library of Congress Control Number: 2011901585

Printed in the United States of America

Dedication

This book is dedicated to Kelsey Renee Vines.
To the life she lived and the legacy she left for
our Lord and Savior, Jesus Christ.

Table of Contents

Acknowledgements   ix

Preface   xi

On Authorship   xiii

Chapter One
The Accident   1

Chapter Two
Kelsey Renee   13

Chapter Three
Our Respective Faiths Before September 2   22

Chapter Four
The Day After   30

Chapter Five
Days of Agony, Days of Prayer   39

Chapter Six
Burying Kelsey   48

Chapter Seven
Rain   53

Chapter Eight
Hard Grief Sets In   72

Chapter Nine
Visits   89

Chapter Ten
A Spring Flurry   107

Chapter Eleven
Sit   125

Chapter Twelve
The Anniversary   134

Chapter Thirteen
Here We Are   145

Epilogue   161

Endnotes   165

Acknowledgements

We want to thank our families for their love, support and contributions to the writing of this story. It was been a group endeavor.

To the Lubbock-Cooper community, who sustained us through those difficult days. Lubbock-Cooper truly is a special place, led by a special man, Pat Henderson, along with his wonderful wife, Jo.

We want to acknowledge the role of our church, Indiana Avenue Baptist Church- specifically, the patient and insightful leadership of Pastor Steve McMeans, and the fellowship we enjoy with all the parishioners. I spent many years wondering what was meant by the phrase "church home." Now I know.

We also want to thank the following for their help in the preparation of this manuscript: Jo Ellen Henderson, who tirelessly edited this manuscript; her two assistants, Katie Heinrich and Sadie Shaw for help with the covers and photographs; friend Jann Freed, who read this manuscript as such; my brother, Jason, who provided insight only as a brother can; and my agent, Carolyn Jenks, for her six years of patient guidance and development on this and other projects, as well. Without them, this book would not be what it is.

Thom Vines

Preface

The greatest fear of any parent is losing a child. On September 2, 2008 that fear became cold, hard reality for us. Our eighteen-year old twins, Kayla and Kelsey, were riding home from basketball practice in their car when a 40,000 pound dump truck swerved into their lane and struck them. Kelsey was driving and was killed instantly. It was the worst day of our lives.

For any Christian the death of a child is a particular challenge for it forces one to decide: do I still trust God? There is no middle road. The loss of a child is so searing that it parts the path of life. It is the proverbial "Y" in the road, and the "Why!?" in one's walk with God. The status quo has been destroyed, and one either emerges from the grief stronger or weaker. One or the other. Our lives were divided into two distinct parts: first, before September 2; second, after.

For us, we emerged stronger, but it was not quick, it was far from easy, and it is still not "over." We now know that it will never be over. The pain we share is a daily challenge. Despite that, we love our Lord more than ever.

I have a Master's degree in psychotherapy from Texas Tech, and I have studied grief from a professional perspective. However, when confronted with the worse kind of personal grief that one can go through, I found there was really only one counselor that helped me, and His name was Jesus Christ.

While each tragedy is unique in and of itself, there are certain common denominators: shock, denial, grief, anger, confusion, and possibly apathy. The particular mix changes with each individual and each circumstance. For people of faith they have the added dimension of trust. Can I trust God again? If He let this happen, does He really love me? Am I somehow being punished? And most importantly, can this type of thing happen again?

After much trial and travail, we each answered "yes" to the

issue of trust. We offer our story as a possible way to help others suffering tragedy and trauma, and emerge from it not unscathed, but still whole in their faith.

Thom Vines

On Authorship

This is our story. The story of a family and boyfriend who went through the single worst tragedy one can face: the loss of a loved one.

Though the words are mine, they really come from us all. Though I carry the narrative, the experience was multiple, and thus, varied. Each of us was thrown onto this journey. Like it or not. We traveled it together, and yet, at times, seemingly alone.

Initially, my thoughts were to have each of us write our respective section of each chapter. It didn't work. It was not fluid. It was disruptive and distracting. So after several drafts and mis-starts, I became the voice, the bearer of the arc of the story. But make no mistake: this is the story of all of us. Each of us has an important part to tell.

Who is "us?"

I am the father, and someone who had to grow into my faith. Those of you who search and seek may relate more to me. Those of you who question and struggle with your faith may find efficacy and meaning in my words, my struggle. You will find that while I have accepted Christ's saving grace, I still have much growing to do. Maybe that describes you. Maybe that describes us all.

There is Becky, my wife of more than three decades, and the mother of our three children. Becky wrote her version of chapter one, and then told me she couldn't do it any more. The plan then was for her to read my chapters and add feedback. She found she could not do that either. It hurt too much. So after that we were left with my probing questions asked as gently and compassionately as possible. For those of you who grieve as only a mother can, she may be your guide. For those who scream, "Why?" she may represent your yearnings. For those of you who do not want to confront and relive, she might be an example of how to cope. There is no one way. Grief is personal. It is individual. And there is no "right way" to handle it.

There is Kayla, who had to find her way through her senior year of high school without her twin. For those of you who have lost a sibling, she can be your example. For those of you who are young, she can represent your searching.

There is Jeremy, Kelsey's older brother. He had already moved out on his own. Accordingly, he was not as much a part of the daily fabric as the others, but his pain was no less manifest.

And then there is John Michael Vestal, Kelsey's boyfriend, Kelsey's soul mate. He chose the verse that headed each chapter. Those of you who already have a strong faith may see yourself in "JM." Those of you who have lost someone who you wanted to spend the rest of your life with may rally to his story. Think of JM and me as bedposts, standing on each side of this tragedy. Each came with a distinct and different perspective. Each reached across the giant chasm to the other. Each grew in one another, and thereby, in Christ. He cannot tell his story without me. I cannot tell mine without him. And so it is with all of us.

This is our story. We pray that it helps others facing the same challenge that we had to face.

Thom Vines

Chapter One
September 2, 2008
The Accident

*"So do not worry about tomorrow; for
tomorrow will care for itself."*
Matthew 6:34

Tuesday, September 2, 2008 was a typical warm and sunny late
summer day in Lubbock, Texas. If the events of that day had not
occurred, I doubt I would have remembered September 2.

It was the day after Labor Day, and I was busy dealing with
construction projects in my role as Deputy Superintendent for
Lubbock-Cooper Independent School District. Around 1:30
p.m. I was walking through the high school gym to check on the
remodeling of the girls' basketball locker room. Both Kayla and
Kelsey had been captains on the team as juniors, and we were
looking forward to their senior season, their last season. Kels was
walking through the gym at that very time. She saw me coming and
broke into a big smile. We stopped and hugged, and then told each
other "I love you." That was the last time I saw her alive.

For John Michael, or JM, as many called him, the final day
began the night before with a Vestal family cook-out on Labor Day.
He picked Kels up, and when he entered her bedroom there was a
song playing on her radio repeating the lyric of "Kelsey."

"What's the name of that song?" he asked.

1

"Kelsey," she said with a smile. "So you can always remember me when you listen to this song no matter what happens, and no matter where I am."

Later at the cook-out, Kelsey told him about her new favorite verse, Mark 5:36: "Don't be afraid, just believe."

As JM later related these stories to us, we all wondered if God was not somehow subtly, subliminally preparing us and her as part of His loving grace. Of course, there is no real way of knowing, but it is a logical question that lingers. Personally, I don't think it was a coincidence.

Indeed, for several weeks an impending sense of doom had been hanging over me. Nothing specific; just the vague feeling that something traumatic was about to happen. And while it was never identified to a specific person or event, I found myself watching Kels very closely when she would walk through the living room.

There would have been a time in my life just a few years ago that I would have said that any attempt to make such a spiritual connection to these events, feelings and thoughts would be wishful thinking, nothing less than a silly superstition. However, by September 1, 2008, I was at least open to the possibility of God's guiding hand in such daily matters.

JM brought Kels home, and there on our front steps they embraced and kissed for the last time, clinging to each other's fingers until that last possible second. It was their last kiss, their last caress. They just didn't know it yet.

On the afternoon of September 2, as I drove home from the office, I came to the intersection of FM 1585 and Indiana Avenue. I looked left down Indiana, and thought: the twins should be coming up that way soon. I felt a slight tug of anxiety. Not a premonition, but just the usual parental fear when their kids were out driving.

I got home sometime after 4:30 p.m., and a few minutes later got a cell call from a school board member, Lanny Lincecum. He said Kayla had been in a car accident, and had been injured. I think I asked about Kelsey, and Lanny said something like, "I don't know." Then added in a voice filled with urgency: "You'd better get out here."

I blew out a breath that was more of a grunt, as fear seized my body like a surge of electricity. I rushed to the scene of the accident approximately four miles away. As I sped down the streets

I prayed, a sense of dread welling inside me. Kayla had been hurt. Why didn't Lanny know about Kelsey? Was she not in the car? If she was, was she okay? If so, why didn't Lanny just say so? Whose turn to drive was it? Wasn't it Kayla's? I prayed: God, please protect my twins.

I thought about calling my wife, Becky, but I was going too fast. I remember Pat Henderson, the Superintendent of Lubbock-Cooper ISD, my boss and best friend, calling me on my cell phone, but I do not remember much of the conversation. By then I was near-frantic. As I reached the intersection of Indiana Avenue and FM 1585, I saw an ambulance going through the stop light heading south. I cringed and sucked in a breath. This is bad, I told myself. This is going to be really bad. My prayers turned to pleas. God, *please* let my twins be safe.

As I sped south down Indiana Avenue, I could see several dozen vehicles. I got as close as I could, skidded to a stop, and ran towards where a throng of people stood. There was a huge dump truck parked at an angle on the wrong side of the road. The dump truck was so huge it completely blocked the view of the Grand Am.

As I ran up, I noticed people turning to look at me. I ran around the back end of the dump truck and saw the Grand Am in the bar ditch. The left corner had been smashed and driven deep into the car. I looked to my left and saw Kayla being put on a gurney. I ran to her, and except for a few cuts and bruises, seemed reasonably okay. I breathed a sigh of relief. Kayla was okay, which seemed like a miracle considering the damage to the car.

I started to breathe more normally and relax a bit. It seemed like we had dodged a bullet, as the expression goes. It certainly could have been much worse. I took notice of who was in my immediate area. There was Pat, two Lubbock-Cooper police officers, Chief Jesse Pena and Lieutenant Rick Saldana, as well as Buddy Cooper, the husband of Sherry Cooper, who worked in our administration office. I learned later that they were the first on the scene, and saw Kayla walking in the field.

As I relaxed a little more, I started to re-orient myself, and it dawned on me that Kelsey was not there. I looked around and did not see her. "Where's Kelsey?" I asked.

There was no answer.

"Where's Kelsey?" I asked again.

3

"...She didn't make it," Buddy finally answered.

"No," I denied. I think a part of me already knew it, and did not want to confront the truth.

Buddy repeated himself.

"No," I said again.

"Yes," both officers said.

I turned, and looked at the Grand Am, and realized for the first time that my daughter lay in that crumpled heap. A sense of rushing came over me, as if suddenly I looked at the car through a zoom lens. The whole world shrunk as I focused in on the car. All I saw was the car and the ground between me and it.

I bolted for the car and they grabbed me. I fought with them. "Let me go to my daughter!" I yelled. An EMT rushed to me. He said a few things I do not remember, and I tried to step around him, but he blocked my path.

I yelled "No," and collapsed to the ground wailing, "No, no..." I moaned over and over. Pat and the others picked me up and tried to walk me to a car, but I could not walk, and folded to the ground. They picked me up again and put me in the back of a car. And there, face down in the back of some stranger's car, I began crying. The first time of many times. The nightmare had begun.

As it also had for Becky. Bec taught first grade at North Elementary, approximately two miles north of the accident site. Principal Rita McDaniel received a call from Betsy Taylor, Lubbock-Cooper's Chief Financial Officer, about the accident. Rita was not told the extent of any injuries. She rushed to Bec's room, and told her to get her purse: the girls had been in an accident. Rita and assistant principal, Mitch Rasberry, drove Becky south to the accident site, parking approximately a hundred yards north where JoEllen Henderson, Pat's wife and Lubbock-Cooper's Director of Public Information, was waiting. Bec got out of the car, and there on a forlorn strip of asphalt got the worst news any parent can get: "It's the girls, and one of them didn't make it."

Becky told me later she knew in her heart it was Kelsey, but asked any way. Becky collapsed to the pavement, shaking, yelling, "No..." over and over.

Meanwhile, I was in the back of a Suburban, my body heaving with cries and wails. This can't be happening, I kept telling myself. It just can't be. After several minutes, I pushed myself from the car, and looked around. Everything seemed surreal. I looked at the Grand Am. Was this really happening? As I look back on it, I was probably in shock. Some people that I do not remember came up to me and said things to me. This is all a vague memory.

Then I thought of Becky. I asked about her, and someone told me she was on her way to the scene from North Elementary where she taught first grade. I saw Todd Howell, Kayla's boyfriend, standing along the road. I rushed to him and hugged him. Then someone told me Becky was in Rita McDaniel's car. I turned and looked at the Grand Am once more, and considered walking to it. By now a blanket had been laid over Kelsey. I paused and looked at the Grand Am and imagined what Kelsey looked like under the blanket. I took a step towards the car, and then something stopped me. I paused, then turned away, and walked north towards Rita's car. In retrospect, I am glad the men kept me from viewing Kelsey, and I am glad I refrained from going to the car afterwards. Some things are best left unknown. Today, in a file, I have the autopsy photographs. I have not, and will not look at them.

I saw Becky sitting in the car, and I knew that this was going to be the hardest thing I had ever had to do in my life. I did not know that JoEllen had already told Becky that one of them did not make it. I blew out a hard breath and gathered myself. Kelsey and Becky had a very special bond. Kelsey was like her, just as Kayla was like me.

Becky looked at me, then plopped her head back, closed her eyes, and said, "Which one?" Even though she knew, I guess she just had to hear it from me.

I leaned in over her and a memory of our wedding day 32 years ago flashed in my mind. I gritted my teeth, and forced out, "It's Kelsey."

Becky shook her head back and forth.

"Kelsey is dead," I said.

"No, no, no..." shaking her head back and forth. Becky wanted them to revive Kelsey. "She's gone," was all I said.

By now the ambulance carrying Kayla had left. Rita suggested we follow it to the hospital. That twenty minute drive to Covenant hospital was one of the longest in my life. I sat in the back seat cradling my stricken wife, telling her to pray, while I kept saying to myself: this can't be happening.

Kayla was brought to the ER. Initially, we were not allowed to see Kayla, and were ushered into a waiting room. I loudly demanded to be able to see my daughter immediately, and a young man with the hospital told me to settle down. All my emotion poured out onto him. "Don't tell me to settle down! I just lost my daughter, you sonuvabitch."

We were taken down the hall to where Kayla was being treated, and informed that her injuries were not life-threatening. She had a friction burn on her right leg and some minor cuts and bruises. Later, we learned she also had possible ligament damage in her right ankle. Overall, she was physically in pretty good shape considering that a 40,000 pound dump truck had just obliterated the car in which she had been riding.

While the doctors and nurses were attending to Kayla, she asked about Kelsey. Becky told her that Kelsey had been killed. She started crying and looked to me for verification. I nodded, and the hard reality of Kelsey's death sunk in just a little bit more for all of us.

Les Howell, Todd's father, went to the apartment of our son, Jeremy, age 24. Les escorted Jeremy to the ER, and I remember Jeremy being surprised by the number of people outside the ER room. Jeremy entered the room and saw Kayla on the table and rushed to her. Then he asked about Kelsey, and I forced the words from my mouth. Once more the hard facts were driven in even deeper. Actually, we were lucky that Jeremy had not found out by watching the local news. We learned later that a DPS officer had publicly announced Kelsey's death before all family members had been notified.

Much of what happened through the night is a jumbled memory. No doubt I have repressed some of it. Writing this forces me to relive the events. Several times I have had to ask God to give me the strength to get it out.

I remember once walking out of the ER room where perhaps a dozen people stood, including Pat and Jo. Someone said something that I do not remember, and I responded, "Kelsey is gone. She was the best of us."

At some point, I asked if John Michael was there at the hospital. I was told that JM was in the waiting room near the front of the hospital. With the assistance of Mitch Rasberry, Bec and I walked to the waiting room.

I entered the waiting room and saw JM. I will never forget the look of anguish on his face. His entire body was wreathing in pain. To this day, that memory makes me angry at what was stolen from him and her.

JM saw us and stood up. We embraced, and I said, "She loved you." He answered, "I still love her."

Also, in the hospital waiting room were April Ehlers and Brandi DeWaters, close friends of the twins, and part of what they called "The Magnificent Five," a half-tongue-in-cheek reference to their basketball proficiency. We embraced, and I think later they came up to Kayla's hospital room. Much of the rest of the night is a blur.

In this day of cell phones news travels fast. The bottom of John Michael's world fell out when he received a call at his job from one of the twins' friends, Paige Sterling. JM worked at his sister's daycare center, and as they did everyday, Kels and he had been exchanging text messages. He told her he loved her and that he would talk to her in a few minutes, and then went outside to play football with the little kids. When he came back, Kels had texted back, "Hey Sweetheart." He texted back, "Hey Sweety," but no return message was forthcoming. He sensed something was wrong and began to pray. He called Kelsey, but there was no answer. I have often wondered what the scene looked like inside the Grand Am: Kelsey crushed, Kayla pulled from the car, while JM's call rang unanswered.

A few minutes later was when Paige texted John Michael, telling him to call her immediately. He did and learned the love of his life had just been killed, and that the God of the universe had allowed his sweetheart to suddenly die.

Later, JM wrote me. "I felt then how I think Christ felt when He heard the news about the death of John the Baptist. He wept for his friend; yes, Jesus Christ, our hope of glory, wept for his friend, even though He knew the eternal plan of salvation. And so did I. Kelsey was not just my girlfriend; we didn't just love each other. She was my best friend; we loved each other through Christ, not through emotions. That's why it was so true and genuine. Cliché?

You can believe that, but I know what I felt and what I was able to live for that year."

He hung up from Paige and sprinted to his truck. Just praying, not crying yet. It was still too unbelievable to cry. He called his dad frantically telling him what had happened. And then in the middle of the road, while talking to his father, the full realization of what was happening hit him with full force. He sped to the hospital while calling his mother. She had a good friend, who was a nurse in the hospital. The nurse had mistakenly told her that Kelsey was going to live, and that Kayla was the one who had been killed. For that split second, he felt relieved, but then he thought of Todd, of how Kelsey would take losing her sister, and pain stabbed him again. He thought of how much Kelsey cared for Kayla, and how they had both prayed for Kayla to come into her own intimate relationship with the Lord. Then he knew if anyone had to die, it had to be Kelsey. Kelsey had the strongest faith. Still, JM wanted to feel relieved and see both of them sitting in the hospital beds with just some bruises.

That hope was fleeting.

He rushed into the hospital, but he did not see any one he knew. There was no one to comfort him, to tell him the truth. Then running into the front room of the emergency room office, came the mother and sister of Todd Howell, Kayla's boyfriend. They grabbed and hugged him, then led him into the same small waiting room Becky and I had first been brought. Sometime after that, Bec and I re-entered the waiting room, and saw JM in utter agony. Our journey in grief together had begun.

After Bec and I left the waiting room, JM crumbled in the corner, hoping that somehow there he could hide from reality, from the pain and agony. But there was no hiding for him or any of us that day. He was alone with his grief, which is to say, that he was alone with God. And there in God's loving cocoon, he asked the question that we all asked: Why!? What could possibly be the purpose of this?

Some time later, his parents rushed into the waiting room, and found John Michael on his knees facing the wall. His mom knelt beside him and hugged him. "I'm so sorry, handsome boy. I'm so sorry." His dad knelt, as well, and began to pray softly over them, as he fought through his own tears. Jordan, JM's little brother, rushed in to the waiting room from football practice. Jordan and JM were not just brothers. They were best friends, and Jordan brought him love that only such a person could.

Good friend, Clayton Walker, then came in and prayed over JM, as did Reverend McMeans, the pastor of Indiana Avenue Baptist Church. It was all so surreal. JM, like us, kept thinking this couldn't be happening. His sister, her husband, and nephew, Cameron, arrived. JM looked up at Cameron and smiled. He saw a little boy with a big future ahead of him. JM smiled because he knew our God still reigned. He didn't know how, but he *knew*. He thought of the story of the children, who were with Jesus on the hillside. Christ said, "I wish everyone were like little children, for the Kingdom of God belongs to such as these." For a split second, he envisioned Kels sitting in Jesus' lap smiling. Then reality pounded once more.

JM looked at his brother-in-law, Josh, who had struggled with his faith. JM told me how the Lord suddenly allowed him to see the true Josh, not the sinner, but the Josh who truly was loved by God, the Josh for whom the Lord had a huge plan. JM pointed at Josh and said "The Lord has a plan for you, my brother. I know you don't believe He does, but I will promise you that He is going to change your life someday."

Then he began to pray out loud. "Lord, I have no idea what you are doing, and I can't see how this circumstance will make me who I need to be, but I do know that Romans 8:28 remains true no matter what the circumstance is." That verse says, "We know that in all things God works for the good of those who love Him, and who have been called according to His purpose." JM prayed for about ten minutes, his heart weary and humble, and yet fervent. He asked the Lord to use this tragedy not for just him, and not just his family and him, but for God's glory so that His name could be lifted up.

After we left JM and others in the waiting room, we started the horrible business of calling family. I asked Pat to call my sister in Iowa, and spread the word to my two brothers. Becky herself called her dad in Myrtle Beach, South Carolina. I don't know how she found the strength to do it. I could not have gotten the words out. JoEllen was already busy organizing many of the details of things that would have to be done over the next few days. For all practical purposes, we became Jo's full time job for the next week or so. I sensed it helped her staying busy. I just know how much tougher it would have been without Pat and Jo taking care of details.

At one point, I heard Pat say to someone that called him: "Well, Kelsey is dead." Is that how it's said, I asked myself. I guess it is. It just seemed odd at the time. Obviously, a large part of me had still not accepted the fact of Kelsey's death. Denial, I would learn, faded slowly and never completely.

Once Kayla was moved to a room for overnight observation, several dozen people came to that part of the floor. At some point, a hospital aide brought up the twins' basketball traveling bags that had been removed from the car. For some reason, seeing the bags hit home even harder the horrible reality of Kelsey's death. I turned from the aide and started banging my head on the wall.

Shannon Henderson, Pat's daughter and Jeremy's classmate and friend from when they were five at Meadow, came to the hospital to comfort Jeremy. For the next few weeks Shannon kept a close eye on him.

Later, JM came up to Kayla's room. Kayla was asleep from the antibiotics and pain medicine. JM touched her arm and then fell to his knees in disbelief. I was told later that Becky and I rushed to him, but I do not remember the episode. By then I was in a daze.

John Michael left the room and went outside of the hospital. There standing in the parking lot alone, he looked up at the moon and began to pray. He asked for help to make it through this, that he needed God to be more to him than ever before. As I look back on this from the perspective of over a year, God undoubtedly answered that prayer.

He went home, and once inside, reality slammed into him again. Photographs of Kelsey and he were all over the house. He ran to his room and grabbed the teddy bear Kels had given him a few months before. She had sprayed it with her huge volumes of Dolce and Gabana perfume, so that even when they were not together, there would be a reminder of her. Now the teddy bear was all that was left. Something tangible. Some thing he could hold.

It hurt too much to be in his bedroom with all the reminders of Kels, so he lay on the couch, held the teddy bear to him, and tried to fall asleep. Not a chance.

His good friend, Brian Valigura, came over and prayed for

him. They talked and asked each other how the Lord could allow something like this. JM told Brian that even though he could not see the Lord's hand in this, he trusted the Lord. He asked God, "How can we say that the Lord is so good and that we trust him only in the times when our lives are great and nothing is going wrong." Did we truly trust him? Do we really believe He loves us? If we did, then we would believe that despite the events of that day.

Usually right before he went to bed, John Michael would read the Bible and then write in his journal. He had done this for four years, never missing a night, no matter how late he got home or how tired he was. He knew that this night could be no different. This night was more important than ever. So he sat down at his desk and took pen in hand. He opened his journal and saw hundreds of entries, some as long as a page, others just a sentence or two. That night the Lord told him not to read, but to pray and seek His face. To break the routine and fall into His arms. So he did just that, but before he did, he wrote one last journal entry. It read:

> *"Today Lord my sweetheart, Kelsey Renee, went to be with You, to be Your princess. Please do something BIG through this. The life she lived was wholeheartedly seeking after growing in You. I'm not going to read tonight, I'm just going to seek Your face and seek after the comfort You have always promised me. God strengthen me so that I may be strong and glorify Your name during this time. I love You, Lord Jesus. Be with us now and start a fire from Kels. Tonight will be my last journal entry in this journal. I will start a new one when that day comes. God, I believe you are going to do a new thing, just as Isaiah 43:19 says, "See I am doing a new thing! Now it springs up, do you not perceive it? I am making a way in the desert and streams in the wasteland." Do something BIG in me in my time of need. I love you Lord.*

Sometime after 5:00 a.m., he finally fell asleep on the couch, only to awaken two hours later. He checked his phone. No calls from Kels. No text saying, "I love you." Just stillness. A confusion and an emptiness that he had never felt before filled him. And yet in this time, he instinctively knew that when you are brought to your knees, it is also a glorious time. For it is then you discover that you can no longer do anything by yourself. And your only alternative is to surrender to the one who can.

Later, John Michael wrote: "September 2, 2008 will forever be the day in between two lives for me. I will always look at my life from two distinct periods, the time before September 2, 2008, and the time after. I know though someday will be a new day, and the hope of my Lord that does not disappoint will bring me someone new, someone who will love me through everything. She will no doubt be a perfect gift from the Lord, and I will someday, whether it's here on earth, or in Heaven, look back on September 2, 2008 and be able to finally see the Lord's hand in everything that happened that day."

Meanwhile, Becky and I were still at the hospital in Kayla's room. Shannon took Jeremy to his apartment. Becky, Todd and I tried to sleep on cots and chairs. We got maybe an hour of sleep, while I cradled Becky's body next to mine.

Our lives were irreversibly altered in an instant, like the snap of a twig. Where there had been one continuous part, now there were two: one with Kelsey; the other without. There is a song entitled "Closer to Love" by Mat Kearney that has a line in it: "We're all only one phone call from our knees.[1]" Obviously, every time I hear that song now I think of September 2, 2008. The worst day of our lives.

Chapter Two

Kelsey Renee

*"Trust in the Lord with all your heart, and lean
not on your own understanding; in all your ways
acknowledge Him, and He shall direct your paths."*
Proverbs 3:5-6

No father is really objective about his own daughter, and I do not pretend to be about my own. That said, I think a very fair statement is that Kelsey Renee was a beautiful, loving, young lady, a gentle and genuine Christian who lived as a witness for Christ. She had much to offer and so much for which to live.

She was born a stroke before midnight on April 7, 1990. Her twin, Kayla, preceded her by only ten minutes. They were almost born on different days. She weighed only four pounds, thirteen ounces, while Kayla weighed six pounds, zero ounces. For much of their remaining life together, that was the way it was to be: Kayla was bigger and taller, and then smarter and prettier. Kelsey very much grew up in Kayla's shadow, and that did not change until just the last few years of her life.

From the beginning, it was apparent that they were very fraternal; different in size, shape, hair color and texture, and particularly personality. Within a few days, we could discern that Kelsey was the more vocal and temperamental. Kelsey could wail with the best of them; so much so that during their first Christmas

when we visited my parents in Iowa, I ... car a pair of gun range ear muffs primarily ... vails. Kelsey would start crying, and I would ... and push a little harder on the accelerator.

About the time when she entered k... an to notice that she was very observant. If we lost something, we would ask her if she had seen it. If we wanted to know something about the look of some place we had been, we asked her. As she got older, she naturally developed an interest in photography, and even had a burgeoning business as she entered her senior year. She just had that natural eye that all photographers must have. Her dream was to be a fashion photographer. I suggested that she and John Michael team up. He was considering a career in the ministry. He could write the books, and she could provide the complimentary photographs. I remember when I suggested that to her, her eyes flashed, and she broke into a big smile. I think she liked that I acknowledged that they would be together.

However, her academic skills lagged. By the end of their second grade year, it was apparent that Kelsey's reading skills were not sufficient, and she needed to be retained so she could catch up. We faced a tough decision: split the twins in their grade level, or retain both, even though Kayla did not need to be retained. After much discussion, we chose to keep them together. It turned out to be the proper decision. Both flourished with the extra time and help.

As they developed through their elementary years and into their junior high years, Kayla was clearly the more analytical one, and Kelsey was the more tender one, which is to say, Kayla was like me, and Kelsey was like her mom. There were exceptions to that, of course, but as a rule of thumb that was essentially true.

Kelsey and Becky's bond went beyond mother-daughter. In a real sense, they were best friends. That is not so much a criticism of Kayla or myself, respectively, but an acknowledgement of what Kelsey and Becky shared. On the day she died, Kelsey completed a questionnaire for her senior project in a class called Senior Seminar. Number eleven: "I've always admired _____ (person) because…" Kelsey completed it as, "I've always admired my mom because she is strong and hard working."

Both Becky and Kelsey were very loving. Both were friendly and outgoing. Both saw the best in others. On the same questionnaire,

Kelsey filled in, "One thing I don't understand is _____" with "rude people."

Both Becky and Kelsey were trusting and, at times, gullible. Both were poor at mathematics, but brilliant at the calculus of people. Both turned their soft side to the world. And accordingly, both bruised easily. Both hated it when they thought someone was mad at them. "Are you mad at me?" Kelsey would say about five times a day. Sometimes she over-reacted to even the slightest of imagined slights. I once heard her say, "I don't have any friends," to which I said, "Oh, Kelsey." If she could have seen how people mourned after her death, she would not say that any more. When Kelsey was killed, as much as I hurt for Kayla, Jeremy and myself, I hurt even more for John Michael and Becky. Their bonds were extra special and deep.

A little more about Kelsey's tender heart: because of her, we took in a stray dog. In the summer of 2007, a Lubbock-Cooper staff member, Terry Stokes, found a box of puppies sitting on the side of the road. The twins were working at the school that summer and heard about these dogs. Into my office they marched, and I knew I was in trouble as soon as they sat down and gave me the sad eyes with the hopeful smile look. Are girls pulled aside and taught this? Kelsey was adamant that we take in one of the puppies, and she described this one that seemed particularly sad and vulnerable. I initially resisted. That worked for about five minutes before I succumbed to the inevitable.

This dog turned out to be one of the most loving, but mentally slow dogs in all of canine history. I named her Abby, short for 'abnormal," based on the scene of the same name in Mel Brooks's *Young Frankenstein* about the abnormal brain. We still have Abby, even though about once a week, I want to get rid of her: she completely destroyed the garden in our backyard. Yet, we keep her because she was Kelsey's dog, and she reminds us of Kelsey's heart. I often wonder if Abby remembers Kelsey.

As I mentioned, Kelsey could also be gullible, so much that one friend, Austin Taylor, once said to her, "You know, Kelsey, gullible is not in the dictionary," and she answered, "It isn't?"

She had an innocence about her, the proverbial faith of a child, and sometimes it manifested as naiveté. Once I took her to see a Lubbock-Cooper playoff baseball game in a town three hours

15

away, which necessitated staying overnight in a hotel. Before we left, I learned that she had invited several of her girlfriends along. I told her that we would have to get two rooms, because I could not stay in the same room with other teenage girls. Her reply was pure Kelsey: "I don't see why not. We're all friends."

Once in speech class, she told the teacher, Jason Salinas, that his class was hard. He asked why. "Because," she answered in complete sincerity, "its based on common sense."

A few weeks before she died, the girls' basketball team took occupancy of their new, remodeled locker room. During a meeting with the coaches, Kelsey must have said something particularly silly because Head Coach Trent Hilliard asked her, "Did you only get a quarter of the brains given to you twins?" Afterwards, instead of putting her name above her locker, he taped a quarter with scotch tape. Kelsey did not see the tape, and commented how amazing it was that the quarter was magnetic. Kayla said later that any one could see the quarter had been taped on, but Kelsey just kept staring at it.

Kayla also told us about biology class. Kelsey had to read aloud from the textbook, and instead of saying "organism" she said "orgasm." The class, of course, erupted in laughter.

Then there is the story of the red pepper, which I did not learn of until the one year observance of Kelsey's death. Coach Christie Parsley told the tale to us and to the others. It was during off-season basketball practice. Kelsey and the other girls were on the floor performing drills when suddenly Kelsey stops. There was something red on the floor. Kelsey picked it up and took it to Coach. "Look, Coach," Kelsey said with a big smile, "a red pepper."

Coach examined the item, and said with a cry, "Kelsey! That is not a red pepper. It is a bloody feminine tissue."

Kelsey cringed and threw the tissue across the floor. "Oh, Coach, what do I do!?"

"Don't touch me. Go wash your hands."

Kelsey turned and ran from the gym, her arms spread out from her body. After that, the rest of the team gave her a large dose of good-natured ribbing, always warning her not to pick up any red peppers. Kelsey would just giggle and go on as she always did.

Kelsey also had a mischievous side, as well. When they were

younger, and Kelsey would get mad at Kayla, she would fake a cry until Becky or I got on Kayla- usually for something it turned out Kayla did not do. Then once we were gone, Kelsey would look at Kayla with the biggest smile on her face and giggle. Kayla would be furious, but could not hold her anger after Kelsey's contagious giggle.

Loyalty was also a hallmark of Kelsey. Kayla may have been bigger, but Kelsey often took on the protector role. If Kayla got knocked to the basketball floor, Kels would rush to her side. "Don't worry, twin, I'll get them back for you." And sure enough, Kels would hunt down that player and foul them. If Kayla was having boy problems, Kelsey was by Kayla's side providing comfort to her and broadsides to the poor boy or the other girl.

Part of Kelsey's insecurity was that most of the time she grew up in Kayla's shadow. Kayla got better grades, was a better athlete, and was the prettier of the two. By seventh grade, Kelsey had a definite inferiority complex. Photographs of her at that time showed the timid smile of an insecure young girl.

That gradually started to change. First, Kelsey excelled at track, particularly in the 800 meter run. This gave her something of her own. Then she got two other things: both on her chest. As a daddy, this gave me a certain measure of consternation, particularly when I saw how some boys would look at her.

By the time the twins moved into high school, they were distinct personalities. Indeed, some people did not know they were sisters, let alone twins. I remember Kelsey saying once, "But I want to be twins." Both played basketball (Kayla was better, but Kelsey was closing that gap); both played volleyball their freshman year (Kayla was on the junior varsity, Kelsey on the 9th Grade team); both ran track (Kelsey excelled a little more there); both had long-term boyfriends (Kayla had dated Todd since the 7th grade, and Kelsey had dated a boy named Kameron for over a year).

As I mentioned earlier, Kayla was generally considered the prettier of the two. However, Kelsey began transforming and was becoming a very attractive young lady. In grades, Kayla's were always better than Kelsey's, but through diligence, Kelsey managed to pass everything, and occasionally made the honor roll. School was hard for Kelsey, but I admired her discipline and effort. I

wish all students studied like she did. The failure list would be dramatically smaller.

As her confidence grew, her personality began to blossom. She could be funny, and even goofy in an amusing way. There is a photograph of her eyeballing the camera behind goggles that gives me a smile every time I see it. I put it on my computer screen saver and it is one the photographs we included in this book. And above all, she became very loving. Almost all the photographs you see of her with someone else, she is leaning in towards them. That became her approach to life, which came from a knowledge that she was loved by the Lord. One of the most endearing photographs of her is giving the two fingered "I love you" sign, with which she became identified amongst her classmates. I also chose to include it in this book.

We did not go to church much in their formative years, which was mostly my fault. I was far from the Lord. In fact, as far as I was concerned during most of the 90's, I had significant doubts that Jesus was truly the Lord. More on this in chapter three.

Despite this, Kelsey had a strong moral center. She tended to see things in black and white, good and bad. I can remember her saying she wanted us to go to church so she could "hear a lesson." Thus, a fair statement is that Kelsey developed a strong faith despite me, not because of me. She taught me, not the other way around. Not many dads are that blessed.

In October 2007, her junior year, Kelsey began dating John Michael Vestal, then a freshman at Texas Tech University. JM is the single best human being I have ever encountered. A genuine and committed Christian. Kelsey fell head over heels in love. The fact I asked him to contribute his memories to this book speaks for itself. This is his story as much as it is ours.

Typical to their generation, they "met" on-line, although Kelsey was always embarrassed to admit it. It was October 14. "I was not a big MySpace guy," JM wrote me later. "I had one, but didn't get on it very often, and that night right before one of my intramural football games, I got on, and I had a message from a girl named Kelsey. Little did I know that this girl named Kelsey Vines would turn out to be my first true love. She had said, 'I know this is random. I'm sorry, but do I know you?' 'I don't think so.' I replied. I then realized that she went to Lubbock-Cooper High School, and I

had known some people out there, so I asked her if she knew them. Our conversation started, and didn't end for a year straight. Talk about a lucky guy. These conversations over the internet lead to texting, then calling, and then finally meeting at Starbucks."

That was three days later. "I'll never forget the first time I saw Kelsey Renee standing in the middle of the Starbucks parking lot," John Michael wrote. "That first moment will be replayed in my mind forever. I was standing underneath a street light, and she was standing in the middle of the parking lot. I whistled at her, and she turned around, and right then I felt the Lord say 'There she is'. I was blown away. It was love-at-first sight."

When Kelsey died, JM closed his eyes, and the memories flowed back to the parking lot at Starbucks. "A peace came over me," he wrote. "I felt her with me."

After meeting at Starbucks, they started to date. They knew nearly from the beginning that there was something special between them. And that something special was a relationship with the Lord. For both of them, He came first. "The Lord was always number one during our relationship," JM wrote. "That is how it has to be if we want our relationships, whether husbands and wives or just friends, to last."

"I'll never forget the first time we kissed," JM wrote. "We had gone on our first date to a drive-in movie. We were lying in the back of my pickup, and not watching the movie, just talking and getting to know each other. I looked at her, and said 'I really want to kiss you right now.' She got this wonderful, lovable smile on her face, and said, 'Then kiss me.' I go back to that moment nearly every day, just remembering what the Lord did for me and blessed me with for a year of my life."

I remember how happy Kelsey was during late October 2007. She had not mentioned JM yet to me (she had told Bec), but I could tell there was a under girding joy bubbling up inside her. She positively oozed happiness. Finally, after about a week of JM coming to the front door, and me seeing a quick peek of him before Kelsey slipped out the door, I told her I wanted to meet him. I instantly understood her attraction: a good-looking young man, mature, intelligent, and polite. I remember telling myself: jackpot.

After that, their days started and ended with each other. In the morning, Kelsey would wake up JM with a call and a playing of the song, "You're my better half" by Keith Urban. It became their song. At night, the last thing Kelsey heard was JM calling her to tell her he loved her. For the first few weeks, even months, after Kels died, JM would wake up still expecting to hear "You're my better half." Sometimes, until her cell phone was disconnected, he would call her number just to hear her voice.

I suppose I should be happy that Kels and JM had their time together. There are many couples that never share a single day like they had for nearly a year. But I would be lying if I said it doesn't hurt, that I'm not mad at what was stolen from them.

Most importantly, Kelsey's faith, already strong, flowered with John Michael. It was an amazing thing to watch them grow together as Christians. She started going to John Michael's church, Indiana Avenue Baptist. It bothered her that I did not also attend.

For JM, Kelsey became the girl in the song, "Does Any One Hear Her?" by Casting Crowns: a lonely, sensitive girl searching for truths, longing for the Lord. In a real way, John Michael became Kelsey's conduit to a stronger relationship with God. And in so doing, he helped her, and she helped him. And He helped both of them.

On the senior project questionnaire, Kelsey filled in "One thing I really believe in is _____," with "Jesus is the only way." And to "I wish I could _____," she completed it with "travel the world and do missionary work."

On the day Kelsey died, teacher Tobi McMillan had the seniors complete another assignment: "Ten Things I'd Like To Do Before I Die." Among other things, Kelsey listed: "start a family, photography, and go to a summer Olympics." But the first two were: "Read the whole Bible" and "Go on a mission trip, but do it for the rest of my life."

Accordingly, after Kelsey died, Sundays became the toughest day of the week for John Michael. He missed Kels coming over every Sunday morning to wake him so they could go to church. While he got ready, she sat in his room and played with his "Kelsey wall," as they called it. Each week they seemed to add a photograph to it.

And the memories continued to build even months after Kelsey died. Kelsey loved to leave notes. On slips of paper, receipts, anything. About five or six months after the accident, JM was cleaning his desk and found a receipt. He turned it over, and there on the back Kelsey had written, "I love you JM" surrounded by about twenty-five smiley faces. And then he noticed that there in the middle of the receipt he had written months before Kelsey touched the receipt a simple, powerful phrase: "There is a reason." And there was a reason, John Michael believed, that he found that receipt on that day in that way. As he wrote me later: "There will be things that the Lord will allow you to see and experience throughout this journey with Him that may mean nothing to the people around you, but they mean everything to you. Cherish those things, write them down, and never forget how far the Lord has taken you even if it just seems like a step. Remember He is for us and not against us."

"Colossians," JM also wrote, "speaks of the Holy Spirit, in part, being a deposit guaranteeing what is to come for us. God left us a deposit, a memory so that even in the times when we lose the person we love the most, we can always look to our deposit, and know that our Heavenly Father has not forgotten what He has taken us through, and where He is taking us in the future. He chose you and me to go through the circumstances we're going through because He is the Alpha and Omega, and He has seen the end from the beginning."

As Kelsey's love for John Michael and the Lord grew, so did her confidence and you could see it in her smile. Gone was the insecure crack in the mouth with the shy eyes. She even commented to me how she now loved her smile. My favorite photograph of her was taken three weeks before her death: a beautiful smile that came from the knowledge that she was loved by her family, JM and the Lord. I count as one of God's blessing that JM and Kelsey had that wonderful time together, and Kelsey knew true love. Some people never experience a day of what they had for nearly a year.

During the summer of 2008 before their senior year, the twins painted for the school. One day in August, they were supposed to be shooting basketballs after work. I called and they were not at the gym. Instead, they were painting their respective rooms. When I got home, Kelsey had stenciled on her freshly painted walls a series of Bible verses, including Proverbs 3:5: "Trust in the Lord with all your heart." Little did we know that in one month's time we would be called upon to discover just how much we trusted.

Chapter Three

Our Respective Faiths
Before September 2

"Faith comes by hearing, and hearing
by the Word of God."
Romans 10:17

As you have already seen, John Michael's faith was rock solid before September 2. But even a faith like his was challenged by the fire of losing a loved one. "I used to tell people," he told me, "who were going through tough times that they needed to just 'trust God.' Wow, was that a huge cliché or what? I learned through losing Kels that if you don't have a clear word from the Lord for someone, then don't preach a cliché statement to them because 99% of the time they don't want to hear it."

And yet, through it all, JM remained true and then grew. He knew that God had been building him up his entire life to give him the strength to get through losing Kelsey. That does not mean he did not grieve. It just means he knew God grieved right along with him. He grew through his grief. He grew through God. "You can't know God intimately or personally until He becomes the basis of your daily life," he wrote later. "Until you are brought down, you do not realize the pieces of you that aren't filled with Him."

On September 2, his life, like ours, was shaken to the core. And yet, he recognized God's relentless love for him. "What an amazing thought," he said, "that the God of this universe is totally consumed with you and me, no matter where we are or where we have come from."

Before he met Kelsey, John Michael described his faith as a religious faith, one dependent upon reading the Bible, which he did prodigiously. "But my relationship was not personal," he said. "It was intrapersonal. I wanted to have the knowledge aspect of the relationship and not the love aspect." Once he started dating Kelsey, he discovered that when you fall in love with someone on earth, you experience His love in the process. "Kelsey's love flowed into me and changed me. It enabled me to see God's love." And after Kelsey died, he understood that not even death could ever separate the love they had for each other.

It was that love of Him that imbued John Michael after Kelsey was killed. It was that love that gave him the strength to speak at the funeral. It was that love to witness to others. It was that love that gave him the wisdom to comfort and counsel Kayla, Becky and me in the months that followed, through those horrible nights when we cried and screamed, "Why!?"

Before September 2, I would describe myself as a "casual, comfortable, crisis Christian." Don't impose too much. Don't really ask me for any significant sacrifice. And in a crisis: hey, God, I need ya to come through for me. In other words, I was more of a taker than a giver, more of a moocher than a sharer. I had the attitude of what's in it for me? And yet, I knew that despite my abundant flaws, God still loved me. Isn't that amazing? Could you keep loving another human being that continually treated you that way?

Becky had a fairly strong faith, in part, because of her close relationship with Kelsey. In comparison to most 18 year olds, Kayla also had a stronger faith than most teenagers, mostly because of Kelsey's influence. Jeremy, like many young males, had a more casual, distant interest in matters of religion.

Of all the family, my road to Christ was the most tortured. While I had been raised in the American Baptist tradition in Iowa, by the time I graduated from Central College in 1976, I had burgeoning doubts about Biblical inerrancy, particularly about the viability of the Sermon on the Mount.

The heart of my doubts centered around what I saw as human

23

nature and our potential for Christian altruism. When I was around twelve, my father laid down a challenge to me: find a single truly unselfish act. I never did, and to this day never have. Only Christ was completely unselfish. But then, He was not your typical human being, was He?

At the time I did not see that Christ could help us mitigate our naturally selfish instincts. Instead, I concluded that since we were hopelessly selfish, then Christianity was not really possible. "Turn the other cheek" and "love thy enemy" became not only impractical, but impossible dictums. I found intellectual justification in the writings of Ayn Rand, who once published a series of essays entitled *The Virtue of Selfishness*[2], along with her mega-novels *The Fountainhead* and *Atlas Shrugged*.

Influenced by Ayn Rand, I concluded that Christianity, with its communal altruism, was completely incompatible with the dog-eat-dog individualism of capitalism. Actually, the Sermon on the Mount was more aligned with the values of communalism (i.e. communism) than competition (i.e. capitalism).

Nor did I see the Bible as the beacon of truth Christians proclaimed it. Instead, it was fraught with myths, fables and errors. The world was not created in six days (as we know six days), and the Noah story was just plain silly: Noah collected a male and female of every species? Come on, talk sense. How could one man travel to Antarctica and bring back two penguins, to Australia and get two kangaroos, and collect two polar bears from the North Pole? Get serious. Even if he knew those lands existed, it would take years to accomplish each trip. Furthermore, he did not even know of the existence of microbiological species, which were the very basis of the food chain. I concluded that the Bible was not to be read literally or to be considered inerrant. At best, it was a general guide that at times was beautifully written.

Furthermore, I *hated* all the talk about predestination and God's plan. Right and wrong only had meaning if we had choice. If we were not free to choose, then we were nothing but mindless puppets in some cosmic play, and holding us responsible for our acts would not be right. I saw believing in God's plan was a mind drug and nothing less than an abdication of personal responsibility. It was cowardice at the highest level. Reading Dostoyevsky, Sartre, Camus and the other existentialists reinforced this belief.

Also, I did not understand the crucifixion, the seminal event of Christianity. How did the actions of one person forgive the actions of others, who were the ones who actually committed the wrong acts? It made no sense to me. I was a former high school principal, and when I meted out punishment as a principal, I always tried to punish the wrong-doer. I would never *knowingly* punish one person for the acts of another. Yet, somehow Christ's spilled blood on the cross was supposed to absolve me and all of humanity of our sins. I did not get it. How did Christ's sacrifice absolve *me*? Furthermore, why did it take violence to wash away transgressions?

Then while preparing a unit for a world history class I was teaching, I came across how the followers of Confucius made him a deity two centuries after the fact. That did it. I quickly concluded that Christians had done the same thing as the followers of Confucius. Jesus was not the Son of God. He was a legend.

During this fall from faith, I was never an atheist. I always figured there was a God. After all, someone or something had to at some point create something out of nothing. Where did the material for the Big Bang come from? The forces? No, there was always a God. He was just not a personal God. And Jesus was just a good man, turned into something he was not by impassioned followers such as the disciples and Paul.

Nor was I an "I-don't-care" agnostic. While I did not know the answers, I cared deeply about discovering the truth. I always believed that answering the eternal questions about if there was a God, and what that meant to me personally, was the reason we were put here. At the time I concluded there was a God, but He was not a God active in our lives. He did not micro-manage the universe. He was distant and aloof. Bette Midler's song "From a Distance" includes the lyric, "God is watching us from a distance.[3]" That captured my attitude completely.

Probably the most accurate description was that I was a deist-there was a God, but not a personal God, not a Christian God. We were responsible for our own meaning of life. We were on our own. Prayers were an opiate, only a weak attempt to be rescued from responsibility, and therefore a waste of time. And yet I occasionally prayed (usually trying to solicit God for some imagined immediate need), which, of course, made me a complete hypocrite.

I had always been something of a cynic. I was fond of saying:

25

"Things have to make sense to me." My favorite word was "bull" and other words that went with bull. I suppose that world view was inevitable in light of my belief in the inherent selfishness of all human beings. Accordingly, I did not trust easily. Being a high school principal only reinforced my distrust of humans. Watching the world reinforced this. Watching myself reinforced this.

Thus, during these years, a turbulence and rage fermented and churned inside me. Often I was on a hair-trigger because I was miserable inside. I deeply yearned for a sense of peace and serenity, but I would not accept any creed or faith that I did not truly believe. It had to make sense. It had to be real. It had to be the *truth*. I did not want a creed or faith just for the sake of something to follow. And Christianity, I concluded, was simply not the truth. The Bible was not inerrant, and Jesus was not the Christ. He was a legend.

However, I also concluded that Ayn Rand was not the answer. Over time her self-absorption and independence ("I live for no man and expect no man to live for me") struck me as a hollow void culminating in the modern disease of narcissism. I did not believe life was all about me. There *had* to be something more. But what?

Two years before Kelsey was killed I became a Christian. It was not an "on the road to Damascus" conversion. Rather, it was more like the transformation of C.S. Lewis: gradual, with starts and stops. In hindsight, at first it was more of an intellectual understanding than a true coming to faith.

What changed me? First, becoming a father myself. In 1984 Jeremy was born, and six years later the twins were born. As they grew older, I knew that I loved them so much that I would sacrifice myself, even my life for them. But how could that be if we are eternally selfish? I realized that this was how God must feel about His children times infinity.

Another turning point came in the form of simple words. In 1996 I was completing a year as the high school principal in Mart, Texas. Our next door neighbor, Tim Watson, was the local Baptist minister- a fine man and a fine family. They are still close family friends. In chapter five and six you will see just how close.

Tim and I had several conversations about my doubts. He was always open and never judgmental. I joined Tim's church out of respect for Tim, and so that my kids would have a church background. I see now that I should not have. I was not really a true believer. It was a lie to Tim, and most importantly, to God, for me to sit there in church and piously bow my head.

In June, Pat Henderson called me to offer the position of assistant superintendent at Lubbock-Cooper. I had been the assistant principal under Pat at Lubbock-Cooper High School from 1993 to 1995. As we were preparing to move back to West Texas, Tim stopped by. He asked me where I stood in terms of my faith, and I answered that I still had significant doubts. He frowned, gave me a hug, and then said six simple words: "Just remember that God loves you."

On the surface, hardly profound and certainly not new; but for some reason those words resonated with me. I think I was just ready to hear them, and coming from Tim, they had a credibility that stuck. I do not know how many times I have thought of Tim's simple message; obviously many, particularly since September 2. The power of simple words.

Another life changing event was the death of my father, which was an unexpected affirming experience. Dad was a Christian man, and when he died I knew he was in heaven. I remember being happy for my dad. The sense of comfort that came over me was a great and wonderful surprise. Maybe I believe more than I think I do, I told myself. I believed there was a God who created the universe, and followers of Him went to heaven.

But was I a follower? No, I had to conclude. Acknowledging the power of God was not the same as worshipping. What held me back were doubts about the nature of Jesus, and I felt something pushing me to answer this question. At the time, I did not see that it was God seeking me more than me seeking Him.

We started attending Aldersgate United Methodist Church, and I started by reading C.S. Lewis's *Mere Christianity*[4]. I loved reading C.S. Lewis. His work was logical and methodical. He distilled the issue of whether Jesus of Nazareth was the Christ into a simple choice. Jesus, he argued, was either Lord (what he said he was); a liar (of tremendous proportion); or a raving lunatic (because he knew what was going to happen to him if he called himself a king and savior). He was not, Lewis advocated, just a good man. A good man would not lie. It was very powerful stuff, but it still did not specifically address my issue. I still thought Jesus was a fourth "L:" a legend.

Impressed with Lewis's intellect, but still unconvinced, I turned to another apologetic, Josh McDowell, and his book *More Than a Carpenter*[5]. McDowell quoted Lewis's three "L" dichotomy, and then asked a simple, but powerful question: "Who would die for a lie?" McDowell pointed out how eleven of the twelve apostles went to their deaths (six were crucified) for advocating that Jesus was the Christ, not just a good man. "Now if the resurrection did not take place (i.e. was false), the disciples knew it." Throughout the sordid story of the human species, many people have certainly died for lies. But they did not think it was a lie. They believed at the time that it was true. They may have actually ended up being wrong, but they *believed* it was the truth, and it imbued them to further endeavor, sometimes to the point of sacrificing their lives.

That fool's paradise does not apply here. The disciples *knew* whether Jesus was resurrected or not. They were there. They saw what actually happened. They saw Christ afterwards. Thomas even stuck his fingers in Christ's wounds. And those multiple observations changed them. Before that several had doubts about the divinity of Jesus, and indeed, on the night of Christ's abduction every one of them deserted the Son of Man. But after witnessing the resurrection, doubts were swept away, and those men were now willing to die for the truth. And die they did, a fact further substantiated by Roman historians, who were hardly friends of early Christianity.

If the disciples had known it was a fabrication, a deliberate creating of a legend and a deity, *at least* one of them would have broke from the pack and spilled the story when faced with the reality of dying on the cross, or by the point of a sword, arrow, spear or stones.

When I read this, I was sitting on my front porch. I remember putting the book down, thinking about it for a few minutes, and then with a jerk I sat up in my chair. It's true, I said to myself. Jesus *is* the Christ! My mouth fell open, and a wonderful swelling swept into my chest and enveloped me. It was the presence of the Holy Spirit. Glory be to God for He forgives us even though we do not deserve it.

I quit reading for awhile (maybe a few days, I don't remember) and just contemplated this wonderful revelation and sensation. It's true I kept repeating to myself. It's true.

So I was saved. I was inside God's tent. However, there was much I still did not understand, much more growth for me to do, much more growth for Christ to activate in me, so much that I really did not understand at that point just how much more. I still had not resolved all my doubts about Biblical inerrancy, was still far too consumed with myself, and treated God like He was Santa Claus. I knew God wanted unconditional surrender, and I was still too weak and selfish.

In the fall of 2007, as Kelsey began dating John Michael, I started putting down some notes for a book on my spiritual journey. I entitled it *From Ayn to Awe*, and completed it in the spring of 2008. I intended to have Kelsey read it some day when she was older and could understand my past doubts. Now the lesson is: don't wait.

Chapter Four
The Day After

*"Blessed are the poor in Spirit for theirs is the
Kingdom of Heaven. Blessed are those who
mourn for they shall be comforted."*
Matthew 5:3-4

We got maybe an hour or two of sleep Tuesday night. Wednesday
I woke up, opened my eyes, and looked around the hospital room.
Then it hit me like a slug in the ribs: Kelsey was dead. Reality
slammed into me with a sickening feeling.

I pushed myself from the cot and looked out the window at
19th Street and at Texas Tech University beyond, and I realized
that this would be the first full day that Kelsey was not alive. More
reality.

Though it was not yet dawn, cars rolled down 19th Street
ushering people to their day jobs. I remember thinking: well, life
goes on, doesn't it. Kelsey may be dead, but the world rolls on. I
turned and looked at Becky and Kayla still asleep. But what about
us? How do we go on?

I started listing in my mind other Lubbock-Cooper school
personnel who had lost children. Darla Dunn, our Gifted and
Talented coordinator, lost a son, Stephen Starch, in 1997 while he
was serving with the Border Patrol in California. Afterwards, she
established a prestigious scholarship in her son's name. Bill Pitts,

who worked in administration with me, lost two sons, possibly both as a result of exposure to Agent Orange during his days in Vietnam as a Navy Seal. Bill's office was next to mine, and I watched his grief up close. Teacher Marla Cook, one of the twins' favorite teachers, lost her Kelsi in 2001 in a car accident not a hundred yards from where our Kelsey was killed. A cross still marks the spot. I remembered how Kelsi's death had played hard on Kelsey's mind and heart. Another loss occurred in 2004. Lubbock-Cooper High School senior, Andrea Rodriquez, was killed in a car accident less than a mile from school. Andrea's mom, Paula, was an aide at our Middle School. An ex-board member, Ronnie Quest, lost his daughter in a flood in the Texas Hill Country in 2006. Ronnie had been interviewed at the time, and had said, "Parents aren't supposed to bury their kids." At Rachel's funeral I watched Ronnie and his family walk out, and I tried to imagine how they felt, but could not. I just hoped it never happened to us. Each time I had said to others about their respective grief: "That's as bad as it gets." Now we were confronted with that horror, that reality, and it was as bad as it could get.

There's a bromide that goes something like, "Today is the first day of the rest of your life." For all of us awakening on September 3, that was no longer a cliché, but rather a harsh and simple truth.

Like us, JM had slept a few fitful hours on the couch, while clutching Kelsey's perfume-sprayed teddy bear in the vain hope that he could freeze out the rest of the world, at least for a while. And like us, he had that split second after waking, and before he remembered. That horrible half second of twilight. Like throwing a rock into the water. For a fraction of a second, the water is pushed back and the rock seems almost suspended in the air above the water. Then the water comes crashing in like the Red Sea on the Egyptians.

Out of habit, he checked his phone. No message from Kels. However, he had dozens of new messages and missed calls. At that moment, he did not want to talk to any one. What could any of them say that would ease the pain?

In Kayla's hospital room, breakfast was delivered. We each ate a few bites, but none of us had much of an appetite. The local newspaper, the *Lubbock Avalanche-Journal* (I never have

31

understood the avalanche part- West Texas is table top flat) was delivered, and in it was an article on the accident. There it was in black and white. Kelsey was dead. More reality.

Pat and Jo arrived. Kayla was released from the hospital, and we were driven home. I sat in the back seat and held Becky. We were silent. We were numb. It all seemed like some bad dream from which we could not awaken. Despair and denial rolled over us in intermittent waves, coming from opposite directions, battering our minds and souls.

When we got home, Kayla's classmates were already there waiting for her. We got Kayla arranged in her bed with her right leg propped up. Despite a regular dose of pain killers, she was still in significant pain, as well as being nauseous from the pills. She spent the next few days essentially in a drug haze.

After Kayla was taken care of, I walked into Kelsey's room and sat on her bed. The night of the accident Becky had returned home to get some things. At that time she had gone into Kelsey's room. "A great peace came over me," she told me. Not me. I sat there on Kelsey's bed, and a horrible emptiness engulfed me. So hollow that I could not even cry. Her absence was palpable. Never again would she lie in this bed. Never again would she sit at that desk. Never again would she put on those clothes in her closet. She was gone. Gone.

I looked at the photographs on the wall of her and friends, of John Michael and her. Pangs of pain and anger hit me as I realized what they had lost. I looked up at the Bible verse she had stenciled on her wall just weeks before: "Trust in the Lord with all your heart." I stared at the words from Proverbs 3:5. Trust? Is that what I am supposed to do now?

I took a shower and washed Kayla's blood from my face and hands. Somehow I felt like I was abandoning Kelsey a little bit more by washing away the blood. As if I was trying to escape. As if going on with even the most routine regimens of life was somehow disrespectful.

I do not know how many times I cried over the next four days, how many times I had to tell myself that it really happened, that it was not some terrible dream. Through those four most horrible days of our lives, days that no parent should ever have to endure, we were supported by family and friends, Pat and Jo, and the

Lubbock-Cooper community. Jo worked tirelessly and galvanized the many people that bolstered and sustained us. We will probably never fully know all the things that Jo and dozens of others did for us. We were all in crisis mode. It was some weird, surreal alchemy of adrenaline and numbness. At times, everything was a blur, and then there were other moments so vivid that I have never been as alive.

From Wednesday morning through the next few weeks, our home, except for bedtime, was rarely without visitors. The support we received was incredible. At times it was almost overwhelming. Occasionally, we found ourselves in a role reversal: we had to comfort them. Becky was particularly attuned to this. They had come to comfort us, and some broke down in the process. Becky picked them up. I was awed by her strength.

This accident and the way it happened understandably shook many parents. Some people would come up and you could see in their eyes a searching. What is it like? their eyes said. You now know a reality I can only imagine. You could see the pleas in their eyes "please God, never let this happen to my family."

Sometime on Wednesday, my middle brother, Jason, arrived from Detroit. The flood gates of our grief opened onto him. Later that day, my sister, Kathy, and her husband Rich, arrived from Iowa. Once more we poured our pain onto them. Each time my legs would go limp as they hugged me.

My mother, who lived in Iowa, had a stroke in 2007 and had lost the ability to speak. She could fully understand what we were saying, but could not reply beyond "yes" and "no." We made the decision to not tell her- no sense adding to her pain that she could not articulate.

Wednesday afternoon Pat and Jo escorted us to Lakeridge Chapel to plan the funeral. Previously, I had always thought cremation made sense, but now I could not bear the thought. Admittedly, an emotional decision. After all, we get new bodies in heaven.

We entered the front door, and one of the managers approached us. I said, "We have to plan a funeral," and involuntarily blew out a breath in her face as the reality of my words flowed over me. A funeral. We had to plan Kelsey's funeral. Was this some bad dream!? Burying my dad was painful, but that was not even close to this.

Becky was adamant that the service celebrate Kelsey's life and faith. We never felt pressure to spend a lot of money as a way to glorify her. She had been about glorifying God, and that was what this service would be, too. Becky also wanted to donate any possible body parts. I think some skin and bone sections were finally donated.

We had to pick a casket. More reality. More tears. Then it was to the cemetery to choose a grave plot. Becky wanted Kelsey to lie in Peaceful Gardens Cemetery because it was just a hundred yards north of Lubbock-Cooper High School. "We can visit more easily," she said. And she was right. Many a day I took a swing by to be with Kels.

For some reason, it was easier than choosing a grave plot than a casket. Maybe I was cried out by that point. Who knows how the mind really works. Grief is a curious thing.

Then came a surprise. "Would you like to purchase plots of your own?" I remembered my head jerked back slightly as the reality of the question sunk in. This was no longer just about Kelsey. This was about Becky and me, where our earthly bodies would lie. I had never considered the question before because I did not have to. Now I had to.

I was dropped off at the Lubbock-Cooper administration office and had my Tahoe brought to me from our bus barn. Tuesday evening when Becky and I headed to the hospital with Rita and Mitch, our Lubbock-Cooper school police had taken care of my car. When I came in the office, the staff came up and hugged me. They did not know what to say. What can one really say? Sorry seems utterly inadequate. I told Sherry Cooper to thank her husband, Buddy, for helping me at the scene. I knew it was a difficult task to tell someone that their daughter was dead.

I drove towards home and stopped at the accident scene. The twins' Grand Am and the dump truck had been removed, of course, and all that remained were a few skid marks and the markings left by the police to investigate the accident. I remember thinking how empty it all looked. I looked at my watch. It was almost 4:30. In a few minutes Kelsey would have been dead for 24 hours. Earlier that day I had been telling myself: Kelsey was still alive at this time yesterday. Within a few minutes, that would no longer be true. For some reason that time differential mattered. I guess it made the finality of death that much stronger.

I returned home to a house full of people and ever mounting piles of food. I remember thinking of the irony of it: all this food at a time that we could not hold much down.

The outpouring of love and support was incredible, and I sensed also that this had really scared a lot of people: it could happen to them, to their kids, just like the snap of a finger. A 40,000 pound dump truck could swerve into them just as easily. The fact that the collision and death had happened so quickly was a small source of comfort to me. The police had told us that Kelsey had died instantly. At least she had not suffered.

Sometime on Wednesday or Thursday, we were told about Matthew 6:34. Seniors at Lubbock-Cooper High School are required to complete a senior project. As part of that, they have a class called Senior Seminar. Each class period one of the students is required to give a short lesson on some topic. Tuesday, September 2, Kelsey had been assigned to give the short lesson, and she gave it on Matthew 6:34. At some point in my life, I may have read the verse because the few times I would read the Bible (usually in my deist days I read it with the orientation of trying to invalidate the Bible), I would start with the book of Matthew because it was the first book of the New Testament. So I may have read it before, but I certainly did not have it memorized.

There are several versions of Matthew 6:34, and my favorite is: "So do not worry about tomorrow, for tomorrow will care for itself." My mouth fell open when I was told that Kelsey had read this to the class that day.

"She knew!" one of her classmates said.

Did she? Maybe. I would like to think that God was softly, subliminally preparing her, and it is quite possible that was precisely the case. But we'll never really know, at least not on this side of the grave. And I suspect that once we are in Heaven, we will be so overjoyed that our earthly questions will no longer matter. The salient thing at the time was that it was another small source of comfort.

Still another source of comfort was a scene I imagined in my mind: my dad greeting Kelsey in heaven. Then I imagined Kelsey greeting my family and me. I also wondered if Kelsey had what has been called an "out-of-body" experience as her soul left her earthly body. Did she look down on the accident scene? Did she see Kayla unconscious in the car? Was she still there when I arrived?

At 6:00 p.m., reality crashed in again like a twenty foot high wave hitting a rocky beach. The local news did a live spot from Lubbock-Cooper High School on Kelsey's death. The reporter showed how the LCHS students had made a make-shift memorial in the Commons area. One of Kelsey's friends, Brandi DeWaters, was sitting next to me, and I grabbed her, and we both cried as we watched the news segment.

In between tears, Becky was fuming. "I want you to get a lawyer!" she demanded.

"We will," I assured. "Let's just wait until after the funeral. Then we can start thinking about those kind of things."

John Michael came over. He walked in with Kelsey's teddy bear held to his chest. Becky and I rushed to him and hugged him. Then he headed straight to Kelsey's room, which was filled with her friends sitting on the bed and floor looking at photographs and sharing stories. Crying. Hugging. He turned and walked into the closet. He opened the dirty clothes hamper, grabbed the t-shirt on top, and collapsed to his knees. For an instant he could smell her. For an instant she was still there. Then he folded into a ball and started crying. Kelsey's friends left him alone, not wishing to invade on the power of the moment. JM pulled himself up and fell on her bed. The future they had planned was gone forever.

He went into the bathroom to look at where his sweetheart would get ready for each day. Kelsey's stuff lay everywhere, just as she had left it, as if it was expecting Kelsey to return.

At this point, I came in. We hugged and cried some more. Then I wrapped my arm around his neck and put my head against his. "I know you can't see this right now, but someday down the road you will meet someone, and she won't be Kelsey, but she will fulfill all you've ever wanted and needed." And then I said, "We want to be invited to your wedding." He looked at me out of the corner of his eye like I was two parts crazy. Then he looked down and said softly, "...No doubt. Not only will you be invited, but you will be one of the first to meet this girl, whoever she is, and where ever she is."

As John Michael prepared to leave, all of Kelsey's friends rushed to him. "What am I going to do?" he said over and over. As he walked out, someone pulled him aside and said, "You know what you are going to do John Michael: have faith." Later, JM wrote me: "Now that I think about the day of September 3 in hindsight, I see that God had built my faith up for that day. He had built a solid foundation so that when that day would come, which was inevitable, I would be able to stand in Him, even if I had no physical or emotional strength left in me."

Meanwhile, I had to get out. The house was becoming ever crowded, so Jason, Rich, and I went to Pat's. Already at Pat's was Ronnie Quest, the former Lubbock-Cooper board member who had lost his daughter a few years previously. Ronnie is the fatalistic type. "Life just whittles you down," he had once said to me. Ronnie and I talked over a few drinks, and it was good to talk to someone who had been there. There were no pretensions or bromides. Just a shared hard and cold reality.

We went home, and an A-J reporter was doing a story for Thursday on Kelsey and asked that I call, which I did. I told him how Kelsey was a genuine Christian. That it was not just talk with her, and how she walked the talk.

Despair and denial continued to roll over me in intermittent waves. Sometime late that night, there was an episode of which I have only a vague memory. I was sitting in a chair in the bedroom and became so overwhelmed with grief that Rich thought I was having a heart attack. He told me that I then passed out from utter grief. Rich and Jason checked me, and then picked me up and put me in bed. I stayed there for sometime (I do not know how long), and then got back up. Rich told me about this in July 2009. I have little recollection of it. I was that distressed, and I guess, that disoriented.

John Michael went home and spoke with his mom, who emphasized that somehow this is all part of God's plan. "People always say that," JM told me. "Say it so much it becomes a cliché. But when you are actually living it, it is no longer a cliché. The truth hits you full force." "For I know the plans I have for you," declares the Lord in Jeremiah 29-11-13, "plans to prosper you and not to harm you, plans to give you hope and a future. Then you will call upon me and come and pray to me, and I will listen to you. You will seek me and find me when you seek me with all your heart."

Later that night, JM's friend, Brian, came over. "I can't believe how strong you are," Brian said. Others had told him the same thing. JM wanted to scoff. He had never felt weaker in his life. "It was because people could see God in me," JM wrote me later. "It had nothing to do with me or my actions. It was just Him. He was displaying His love and power through me in the darkest hour of my life. This began a thought process in me of how great our God truly is, and how glorious was His plan even in the midst of this valley."

"September 3, 2008 was a day of a new beginning, but I couldn't see that then. To me it was the end of something, but God has since reminded me that with every end there is a new beginning, and the new beginning is always with Him."

Chapter Five

Thursday and Friday
Days of Agony, Days of Prayer

"But he said to me, 'My grace is sufficient for you, for
my power is made perfect in weakness.' Therefore, I
will boast all the more gladly about my weaknesses,
so that Christ's power may rest on me. That is
why, for Christ's sake, I delight in weaknesses, in
insults, in hardships, in persecutions, in difficulties.
For when I am weak, then I am strong."
2 Corinthians 12: 9-10

"Over the course of these two days," John Michael later wrote me,
"the Lord taught me how to pray. We think of praying as asking
for something we want and some times getting it, and other times
not. But prayer is actually much more than that. This was the
beginning of my truly personal and intimate relationship with the
Lord, and I learned that it is not until you desperately need the
Lord that it truly becomes personal. And it is He that brings the
intimacy to you."

Meanwhile, I prayed for strength to get through these next few
days. After that, I did not know what would happen. And at the
moment did not care. I just wanted to get through the funeral.

Despite taking two Tylenol PMs, I only got about three or
four hours of fitful sleep. I went in to check on Kayla, who had to

sleep on top of her bedspread because she had to keep her right leg propped up. During these horrible days, as we nursed Kayla's physical wounds, Todd did not leave Kayla's side day or night. Kayla pleaded with us to let him stay and sleep next to the bed, and we let him.

When my father died at age 74, Jason, Greg and I held an Irish wake. Each opened a beer, stuck a strip of gray tape on the bottle (dad put gray tape on *everything*), and we told stories of dad. It was wonderfully therapeutic. But after Kelsey died there was no such catharsis. We were too stunned. It was too surreal. It hurt too much.

As much as anything, Kelsey's wake was held publicly in the media. The front page of the A-J on Thursday, September 4, had a large spread on Kelsey entitled "Too Soon." There were several photographs and comments by myself and others. Everyone noted Kelsey's genuine love for God and for others. Over the next week or so there seemed to be some kind of article nearly everyday about Kelsey: the obituary, the funeral, or extracurricular events being canceled at Lubbock-Cooper, and then resumed. It had all become a public event, and accordingly, there was very little privacy, nor time to sort one's thoughts and feelings, which is very important to me. I like to take time to reflect and organize my thoughts, put them into nice, neat compartments. But there was nothing nice or neat about this. My mind was in complete disarray. I was not so much angry as bewildered. I think I was in too much pain to be angry. Yet.

The house continued to be full of supportive people and ever more food. Campuses took turns providing meals. The amount of food piled up so much that I started telling people that if they came in, they could not leave until they ate something. I called it the "Hotel California" rule ("You can check out any time you want, but you can never leave"- without eating)[6]. I was only half-kidding.

Despair and denial continued taking turns lashing my mind and soul. At one point Thursday morning, I stepped out of the front door and walked down the sidewalk. I stopped several hundred feet from the house, thrust my arms out, looked up, and in a silent cry asked, "Why!?" Why did she have to die when she had so much to live for? Why did she have to die when she could have been such a wonderful witness for Christ? Had so much more she could do.? Why God!? Why!? It made no sense.

I think it was sometime on Thursday that Darla Dunn stopped by and talked to Becky and me. Darla had lost her son, Stephen Starch, in 1997, and had established a scholarship in his name. Darla took Becky and me aside and talked to us about what we might expect in the next few days, weeks and months. She said, "In time, you will move into a new normal. You don't know yet when or what that will be, but it will come in time." Of all the things said to us during those horrible days after we lost Kelsey, I think Darla's were the most powerful and most helpful. She had credibility. After all, she had been where we were now.

I thought of Dixie Sellers, a former choir director who had left Lubbock-Cooper when she was diagnosed with cancer. Dixie was another genuine Christian, whose choir concerts were so overtly Christian that Pat and I wondered when the ACLU was going to come in and slap an injunction on us. After Dixie resigned, she came into the administration office and bid all good-bye. I remembered her saying, "But don't worry. Christ is still on His throne." I don't know if my mouth fell open, but I was awed and a bit ashamed. I openly doubted whether I could respond to a similar crisis with such a deep, unwavering faith.

Now I was in such a crisis, and I asked myself: well, *is* God still on His throne? I did not have an immediate answer.

That afternoon Reverend Steve McMeans of Indiana Avenue Baptist came to our home to plan the funeral service. We sat in Kelsey's room, and we showed him the Bible verses she had stenciled on her walls. I added that "from a strictly cold and logical perspective, if this *had* to happen to one of the members of my family, Kelsey was the logical candidate. She was the one of the truest faith. Therefore, she was the one most ready." I think my hard, analytical viewpoint startled him a bit. I know it did me.

Before we spoke, Becky had mentioned to Reverend McMeans that I had written a book about my faith (*From Ayn to Awe*). I was not pleased with this release of personal information because at the time I liked to keep my writing to myself. However, since the genie was now out of the bottle, I said, "Yes, and now I will probably have to add a chapter on Kelsey." Reverend McMeans replied, "You may have to add several chapters." I did not suspect at that time that it would grow into a book of its own.

I told John Michael that if he wanted to speak at the service he could. He did not have to, but if he wanted to, then the opportunity was there. I knew I could not without imploding on stage. Becky felt the same, as did Kayla and Jeremy.

My youngest brother, Greg, arrived with his family. Once more we poured our grief out onto them. Later that afternoon, we took all the family members to the accident site, then to the high school to see the memorial the students had put up in the Commons, and finally we visited Kelsey's basketball locker that had been decorated with flowers and notes from friends and teammates. I noticed Becky became very quiet at this point. Kayla later told me that when she saw these notes and items, she felt the first sting of survivor's guilt with the attending question: why was I spared?

As part of the bond construction, I had redecorated the locker room that summer, and we put in red and black carpet squares (the school colors). Before the school year began, Kayla and Kelsey, as senior captains, chose their lockers. Kelsey saw the floor, and said, "Oh, we can play checkers," and proceeded to jump around the room. As I stood in the locker room with my family, the memory of Kelsey playing checkers on the floor just a few weeks ago brought back a smile to my face. I looked up, and there above Kelsey's locker I saw two quarters. Coach had added a second quarter. I smiled and knew Kelsey would have liked that.

The only things I remember about Thursday night were that the house was full of wonderful people, and John McCain gave his acceptance speech at the Republican National Convention. I was a political science major in undergraduate school, and I taught Government and Economics during the teacher portion of my career in public education. Normally, I would have listened to the speech very carefully. But that night, I just could not focus on McCain's words. I remember thinking that this was just another example of how life went on.

Friday morning Kelsey's obituary that Jason had written was in the A-J. Betsy, Jason's wife, arrived from Detroit, as did Tim Watson, his wife Jann, and daughter, Kelly, who was the twins' age. The Watsons were very dear friends. In chapter three, I recounted how Tim had helped me with my spiritual struggles. He always seemed to magically appear in times of crisis. When my dad had his heart attack (he died the following day), Tim just happened to have been in Lubbock. Before we left for the all night drive to Iowa, he gathered us together for a prayer, a prayer that was very comforting in preparing us for our loss. Now he was here again to help with the funeral service of our daughter.

The house was filled once more with caring people, most of who seemed to bring food. I still could only nibble on a few carrots.

That afternoon Pat and Jo took us to view Kelsey's body. Personally, I knew I had to see her. It was a step I knew I had to go through. Becky and Jeremy felt that way, too. "It's closure," Becky said. "I didn't see my mother after she died, and there was always something missing afterwards." Later, Kayla said she wished she had never seen Kelsey in that state. Still, as tough as it was for all of us, I think it was necessary, a rite of passage in the journey of grief. It turned out to be one of the toughest things I ever faced. We walked into the viewing room and I could see Kelsey's solemn, frozen face protruding just over the edge of the casket. She was under heavy make-up. There were scars, and she looked older. I lurched towards her and put my hands on each side of her face.

"Be careful!" Bec said, grabbing my wrist.

I sat down, and at one point was crying so hard that I choked myself. Lakeridge Chapel had put together a video collection of photographs of Kelsey. It was very tastefully done, but at that particular moment it only drove home harder the reality that Kelsey was gone.

We had to decide if the casket would be open or closed for the funeral service. I initially thought it should be open; that way would help bring closure to the students. However, others suggested it would be better closed and to remember Kelsey the way she had been. For the kids, actually seeing her may have been too much to take. I did not have strong feelings about it, so we went with the closed casket.

Meanwhile, John Michael left home for the chapel. For two days, he had been asking himself if he was ready to see Kelsey's corpse. "Did I really want to see Kelsey when the true girl I knew wasn't in the flesh I would be looking at?" he told me later.

As he arrived at the chapel, the song "Feels Like Home," by Chantal Kreviazuk, was playing on the radio[7]. It was one of Kels's favorite songs. In fact, she had told him "It is my song to you." JM had chosen it for the funeral service. Now here it was playing again as he prepared to see her one last time. He barely had the strength to push himself from the car.

When they entered the chapel, we were already in the viewing room, so JM, his mom and dad sat down on a bench. He desperately wanted his brother, Jordan, there to support him, but Jordan had a football game in Amarillo and had already left.

A short while later, we exited the viewing room. As I left, I turned and looked one last time at Kelsey, then pushed myself through the door. I saw JM and rushed to him. We hugged and cried for a few minutes, and then I said, "Are you ready to see her?" He looked at me a little weird, like he did not understand the question. His mom, Shelley, interceded. "I am going to go in first, and then I will come out to get you."

JM sat back down on the bench for what seemed like half an hour. In actuality, it was only a few minutes. Shelley returned crying. "I'm so sorry," she said to him.

John Michael ran to her. "What? What are you sorry about?"

"You don't need to see her like that," she said. "You need to remember how she was before all this. JM, that's not her. The real Kelsey is not in there. That is just her body."

John Michael became irritated and began to cry harder. "I want to see her!" he said loudly, even though he could hear the Lord counseling: just remember how she was, not what she looks like now. He fell back into the bench and cried for a few more minutes. I told him we were returning home, and that he could stay in there for as long as he wanted. Shelley had asked that the casket be closed, and we accommodated the request. Then I asked the chapel director to let John Michael stay in there with Kelsey for as long as he wanted to.

"I walked into the room along with my mom and dad," JM wrote me later, "and there it was the casket that held the body of the girl with whom I had fallen so madly in love. I remember my mom walking over to the casket with me asking me if I wanted to touch her hair and hands. I said yes, it was the closest thing I could get to having her back, so absolutely I wanted to do it. My mom opened the upper portion just a tiny bit so I could put my hand and arm into it. I felt her hands, and held them for a few minutes while I prayed over and over again. Finally, I let go of her hands and ran my fingers through her hair. When I felt her hair, it made me think of those many nights we spent together in love never even thinking about a day like September 2 ever happening. I spent the next few hours right next to the casket in a chair just holding her hand."

Some time around 6:30 p.m., one of the chapel workers entered the room, and informed him that they had to get things ready for the viewing at 7:00 p.m. "So this was really it," JM said. "The last moment I would ever get to touch my Kelsey Renee. I wondered if the worker knew that."

By now, emotions were cascading through him, as they were through all of us. Pain, denial. Even hope. "I think God is going to do something big through Kelsey," John Michael told me that night.

We went home from Lakeridge Chapel, and I started having chest pains. My brother, Jason, was outside, so I gave him the car keys and told him to very quietly drive me to the doctor. I did not want to create a panic. When I checked in at the clinic, there was one person in the lobby. I told the receptionist I was having chest pains, and I was immediately escorted to a room. I was given a nitro tablet, and it seemed to help. The EKG came back normal, so the nitro pill had served simply as a placebo. I felt a little stupid - not a new experience for me. The doctor was aware of our family loss and told me, "Your heart is broken, but otherwise, in a physical sense, it is okay." I thought that was a really good way of saying it. He wrote out a prescription for valium. I had never taken it before, and I asked how many should I take. He told me to take only one at a time. "If one is not enough, then take another later. If you take too many, you will simply go to sleep."

As we were leaving the clinic, Pat rushed up in his car. "What happened!?"

"How did you know we were here?" I asked in reply.

The one person in the lobby worked for one of the Lubbock-Cooper board members. He called the board member, who called Pat, who rushed from his exercise workout. It was a testament to how public the loss of Kelsey had become. I was a little shocked by it. When Jason and I got home, Bec asked, "Where'd you go?"

I told her, and she got a little mad at me for not telling her. I can't say that I blame her.

Friends continued to visit, including Stu and Karen Cooper and Jim and Peggy Eubanks. I had coached with both, and it was hard to see them in our state. I enjoyed their company so much, and seeing them now served to accentuate just how miserable we were.

That night came the visitation at Lakeridge Chapel. Hundreds of people came to express their sympathy and pay their respects. People that meant something in our lives, that had shared parts of our lives over many years. Friends, colleagues, classmates, former students from Lubbock-Cooper, Meadow and Garden City (other schools at which we had taught). Young and old, old and new, some that we had not seen in years. With my brothers and sister standing behind us, providing support and things like bottled water and a chair upon which to periodically sit, Becky, Jeremy and I stood and greeted people for over two hours. Kayla was sick from the pain medicine and had to lie down in another room. Les and Paige Howell tended to her.

I think all of us got on auto pilot as the people paraded by us. Many did not know what to say. You could see it in their blank stares searching for an answer. In their cringed faces empathizing with our pain. Some fumbled for something to take away our pain, offering advice and hints. We politely listened. They meant well, and at that moment that was what mattered. The night was exhausting, but invigorating at the same time. The wave of support and outpouring was wonderful and inspiring.

During the visitation, Bill Pitts came by. I remembered when Bill lost his first son, he had told me he had never been through something that controlled his thoughts every second like this. When he looked at me, I could tell he knew the pain I was in. There is a bond between parents who have lost kids that goes beyond words.

Also coming by was a classmate of Kelsey's named Chance Bretz. Chance told us that Kelsey had offered her Bible to him last year, and he had refused. Then during the first week of school, Chance asked her if the offer still stood, and she beamed a smile and gave her Bible to him. That night, he asked Becky and me if we wanted her Bible back. "No, you keep it," Bec said. "You wear it out," I added.

There was one distasteful incident. An attorney came through the line and gave us her card. Ambulance chaser. Classless.

After the last of the line had finally paid their respects, we went outside. Several hundred Lubbock-Cooper students had formed a candlelight vigil. They saw us exit the building, and they opened a path to the middle. We walked to the middle, while Todd pushed Kayla on a wheelchair. They gave us lighted candles, and I publicly thanked everyone for their wonderful support during that night and the previous three days. I don't fully remember what I said. Then we left. I did not know that the news was there until they ran a live spot on the ten o'clock news.

By now my brothers and sister and their families were pretty impressed with West Texans and the Lubbock-Cooper community, in particular. Several commented on the massive support and outpouring of love. Greg said, "Now I get it. Now I know why you have stayed here. You found a home." He got that right. West Texas may be geographically ugly, but it has beautiful people.

Two hours north, Jordan, John Michael's brother, dedicated his game to Kelsey. He had ten tackles, two interceptions, one which he returned for a touchdown to win the game.

Later that night, I sat alone in my den and looked up at the Beatles poster that Kelsey had bought me a few weeks before she had died. Then I looked at the A-J article on her. I thought of Dixie Sellers again and what she had said about God still being on His throne. Well, is he? I asked myself. I contemplated the question for a few minutes, and answered I still don't know yet.

Chapter Six

Burying Kelsey

*"For I reckon that the sufferings of this present
time are not worthy to be compared with the
glory which shall be revealed in us."*
Romans 8:18

How does one deal with waking up and realizing that today you
bury your daughter? We got ready, and I remember while blow
drying my hair, I thought: what does it matter what my hair looks
like?

Kathy could not find her purse, so I drove her to Lakeridge
Chapel to look for it. On the way back, a hearse passed us. I read
Lakeridge Chapel on its side and realized that there went Kelsey
heading for the church. Within a few hours, her corpse would be
underground forever. When I got home, I took a valium.

To his surprise, John Michael awakened filled with a strange
sense of joy that he knew had to come from the Lord. A special gift
on an extra tough day. Despite only a few hours of sleep during the
last four days, he suddenly had the energy of a young child. He got
up and quickly dressed, anxious to get to the church.

He later told me that he knew that this day, as hard as it was,
the Lord had big plans for him to share with people about the life
of his first love, his other half, as he had come to think of her;
about sharing her life with everyone, someone who exemplified the

life of Christ on this earth. "If there were two aspects of God that Kels exemplified the most, they were love and a childlike faith," he said. Then he quoted Jesus in Mark 10:15: "I tell you the truth, anyone who will not receive the kingdom of God like a little child will never enter it."

"Kelsey," JM went on to say, "believed in her 'daddy God.' God was not only able to do anything, but He was also willing. We had always talked about God being able to do anything, no matter how hard or how easy." Now he could see Kelsey sitting in God's lap, the eternal child, fully knowing that her "daddy God" could do anything.

The funeral was at 11:00 a.m. We congregated in a side room at the church. Waves of despair and disbelief flowed over me. The valium did not seem to be working, so I took another. It was a mistake. JM arrived and came over to hug us. Then he moved to another room where the four speakers at the service were to congregate. There in that room new emotions reared: sorrow and anger. He struggled to throw off these feelings. He was about to speak to 1,200 people about his sweetheart's love for Christ and Christ's love for us all, and he was not in the right frame of mind. He prayed for God's help.

As he and the three other speakers prepared to enter the sanctuary, he scanned he large room. The place was full. There were more people there on that day than he had ever seen on any Sunday morning. JM knew this was a perfect opportunity to show how God changes lives. Would Kels have wanted it any other way? he thought.

We were told it was time, so we lined up to walk into the main room. Everything was going on a schedule, like some play, and we had parts to perform. I stood at the door and looked at the large room filled with over a thousand people: people I knew, people with whom I had shared experiences. Is this really happening? I asked myself.

The song "Legacy" by Nichole Nordeman was playing, which JM had chosen[8]. As the song played, John Michael looked around and saw so many people he knew. Then looked up at the power point on the screen, images of Kelsey flashing by. "Are you ready?" the Lord whispered to him.

The second valium was kicking in and everything was turning

fuzzy. I was given the signal to walk in. I took a few steps and swung my arm behind me to get Bec's hand. A memory of our wedding flashed through my mind when we were walking down the aisle. I got Becky and Jeremy situated in the front pew. Kayla was in a wheelchair, so it took longer for her to get to her place.

I looked up at the dais and saw JM holding Kelsey's teddy bear. The service began. Tim Watson rose and said some opening remarks and gave Kelsey's biography. It was good to once more hear his voice from the stage.

Then John Michael rose to talk about his Kelsey Renee. As he walked towards the podium, a moment of sadness and pain jabbed him. He looked at Becky, Kayla, Jeremy and me, and knew he had to do this. Somehow. He prayed to God for the strength. He prayed to be reminded of the hope Christ gave the world. That He gave specifically to Kelsey. He asked God to invade the room.

By then I was in a drug fog. Weeks later when watching the video of the service, I realized that I had been out for about two minutes of John Michael's part. I had no recollection of the words I heard on the video.

He talked of how they met. He mentioned her ability with a camera. And then he came to her faith. "I got to witness Christ transform someone's life in such a short span, and I got to be part of walking with her hand-in-hand down this journey. The last few days have been the hardest of my life… People…have told me how my sweetheart impacted their lives… God has a huge eternal purpose, and why my Kelsey Renee had to go, I don't know for sure, but what I do know is that God will be glorified, and His purposes will remain forever. …I am so lucky to have been with Kels the last eleven months, and to watch His eternal purpose in her life take full flight, and see Christ impact hundreds and thousands of lives through my sweet, tender-hearted Kelsey Renee. I believe that the Holy Spirit has a purpose and a destiny for everyone here, and I know that is why all of you came…to say goodbye to our Kelsey, and mourn with us. …God has been waiting for this moment where He could use a tiny, sweet girl to change thousands of lives." Then he quoted Mark 5:36, "Don't be afraid, just believe."

Despite the pain that surged through him, he kept it together. When I heard the speech again a few weeks later, I marveled at it. I admired his strength that came from his faith, which, in turn, made me even more sad at what was lost between them, at what could have been.

Coach Hilliard, the girls' basketball coach, spoke next. After a few indiscreet things about my native Iowa, he told the story of the quarter above Kelsey's locker, which got a chuckle from the audience.

Alexandra Nanny, a close friend of Kelsey and President of the Lubbock-Cooper student body, rose to eulogize. She spoke of Kelsey's witness for Christ, mentioned Matthew 6:34, and mixed in some humorous stories about Kelsey. I remember feeling good after she spoke.

Then came Reverend McMeans' turn. I had never heard him speak before. He talked about seeing Kelsey's room and the verses she had stenciled on her wall. He quoted Proverbs 3:5: "Trust in the Lord with all your heart," and then he completed the verse, "And do not lean on your own understanding." I had never heard that part of the verse. The more I thought of it, the more I concluded that it was the most important part of the verse. "Do not lean on your own understanding." Even in my distressed and drugged state, I could see that it was a key to trusting. I did not know it at the time that I had turned a corner. However, neither did I know how many corners there would be on this crooked, jagged road.

The service concluded, and as we walked out, I patted the coffin. Pat and Jo drove Becky and me to the burial site. To show you how drugged I was, for months I remembered the drive to the cemetery being done by Tim and Jann Watson. I even thought I remembered conversations with them.

Jeremy, Kayla and Todd went in another vehicle. The police escort was supposed to end at the city limits of Lubbock, but continued on to where we turned to the cemetery. As we arrived in the cemetery, there was an honor guard standing at attention for another service. They turned and saluted, and we were deeply touched. At the end of the service, two doves were released. They swirled around over us and then flew off towards Lubbock-Cooper High School approximately a hundred yards away. "Look," Bec said. "They flew towards the school." I smiled as I watched the doves disappear over the school.

Most of the rest of the day was filled with some type of social function, which in America means food and drink- and we wonder why obesity has become such a problem. The purported function of the activities I am sure was to keep us occupied and had the best of intentions. I suspect Jo was the head organizer of this. There was a meal back at the church. I could not eat. We went to Pat's. I could drink. Then to Sheridan's for custard style ice cream. I felt guilty eating custard while dirt was being shoveled over my daughter. Then off to Les Howell's (Todd's dad) for margaritas. That I could handle again. Later, we returned to our home, now not only filled with people and more food, but dozens of bouquets from the service. All through the rest of that horrible day, I felt an anger bubbling inside me that I masked with a feeble smile that was more of a grimace.

Chapter Seven
September
Rain

*"So humble yourselves under the mighty power of God,
and at the right time he will lift you up in honor. Give all
your worries and cares to God, for he cares about you."*
1 Peter 5: 6-7

Like all parents, we had always feared this precise tragedy. It is the
dread of every parent each time their child drives, each time their
child goes out for the evening. You don't really rest until they are
home. Of course, we knew other parents who had lost children,
particularly to car accidents, and each time it happened, I had said,
"That's as bad as it gets."

Now it had happened to us, and I could not believe it. I kept
expecting Kels to walk through the front door as if she had been
on a trip, as if the whole thing had been a bad dream. Denial is a
powerful mind drug, an ego defense mechanism. Freud knew of
what he wrote.

All parents worry about their kids: grades, friends, the teenage
years, college, career, and spouse. The irony was that I never spent
a great deal of time worrying about the twins. Both were very
grounded and mature, and then later each had solid boyfriends
(Todd and JM) that treated them like ladies. And if nothing else, I

figured the twins always had each other. Being a twin was a kind of a security blanket. Or so I thought.

The death of a child instantly re-orders one's priorities. Things that used to seem so important, no longer carried much concern. Where would we go on vacation? What would prom dresses look like? Would Kayla be All-District again in basketball? Would Kelsey make it this time? Would one of the twins be on the homecoming court? Who won the presidential election? Who won the World Series or Super Bowl? How gray was my hair? How white were my teeth? All that seemed suddenly trivial. All that mattered now was taking care of my family.

I remember wondering if six months from now my sense of priorities would to some degree revert. At that time I did not see how. More importantly, I sensed that there was already a part that did not want to go back. A new reality had set in. I did not yet understand it, but it was fundamentally different, and there was no going back.

And what was driving this sense of no return was a conviction of which I was barely aware. It was really more of a sense, a feeling, rather than a didactic thought. Like being aware of the presence of someone, but not actually seeing them yet. The conviction? This was all somehow part of God's plan. I don't know how I knew it at the time, but down deep I knew it was there. I was not *hoping* that it was there. I *knew* it.

I also noticed that our identity changed. No longer were we the family whose father was the Deputy Superintendent. No longer were we a family with twin seniors who would figure prominently in the school year. Now we were the family that had lost a daughter. That was how everyone looked at us. That's how we looked at ourselves.

It was Kayla's senior year. A "normal" experience was now out of the question. We had to make the best of it and take one day at a time. We never had a family discussion about how we would act in public or private. I think each of us individually decided not to make a histrionic display. That was not us. So we did not wear our grief "on our sleeve." We didn't have to; it welled out on its own.

All humans have choices in their conduct. We could go on as best we could, or we could implode. For us there was not that much of a decision to make. We muddled on, often feeling like we were on autopilot in a thick fog, but on we went. Many people have told us how strong and courageous we were. I really don't think that was what it was. It was not so much courage as the absence of an acceptable alternative. We went down this path because it was the only one in front of us that made any sense. I knew I had to lead by modeling. If they could see me surviving, then in time, it might get better, or at least more tolerable.

Since the accident, we had been focused on the funeral, and there was a natural sequence to things. Now that had come and gone, and we were left wondering what was next? By nurture I was a planner. Take responsibility, set a goal, make a plan, work the problem: that was my daily modus operandi as a school administrator. However, after the funeral, that did not work any more. I was diffracted and diffused. Jo stepped in and helped us organize the details that had to be done: death certificates, probate court, insurance details, so forth. I remember staring at the death certificate. It made it so official. So final.

Sunday, the day after the funeral, was a hollow day punctured by piercing stabs of anguish that bled into a fog of denial and disbelief. Several times that day I had to tell myself that it really did happen.

Family left, we cleaned house, and I sat down to finish a letter to the Lubbock-Cooper staff, and then one to the student body. As I was composing my thoughts, I remembered Dixie Sellers and her comment that God was still on His throne. Well, I asked myself again, was He? Was God still on His throne?

I contemplated the question for several minutes and decided yes, God was still on His throne. After all, He was the creator of the universe through some process I did not understand. I had never fully accepted Genesis or evolution at face value. At some point something had to be created out of *nothing. What* could do that?

So there was a God, a supreme being that created the universe. I believed that before Kelsey died, and I still believed it after. But I knew that believing in a creator was different than believing in a personal God. Supremacy was different from trust. I may have acknowledged that God is the supreme power in the universe, but that was not the same as trusting. Kings sat on thrones and were the supreme rulers of their land, but that did not mean they were infallible. Being supreme was not the same as being right. Was God right? Was God to be trusted? Or was God to be obeyed simply because He was supreme? I didn't know.

Once more I was flooded with the same questions. Why did He let such a horrible, senseless thing like this happen? Were we being punished for our sins? Did Kelsey's loss mean we were now immune from further such tragedy? Or could this happen again? Was there some quota on tragedy? And just what did it mean to truly trust? At this point I had few answers, just questions.

That afternoon I got a call from Deena Weeks, the parent of a Lubbock-Cooper student. In the past, she and I had several confrontations over student discipline. I could not believe that she was calling my home on the Sunday after burying my daughter. I gritted my teeth, and braced myself for the onslaught, as I felt anger swell inside me. But I was wrong. I had jumped to a conclusion. She and her family had made a cross, and they wanted to give it to us. I was so surprised that I think my mouth fell open. A wave of guilt flowed over me.

About an hour later they arrived. The cross was beautiful and huge. Standing a full six feet high, it had a white marble veneer, and in the middle was a photograph of Kelsey at her last prom with the verse Matthew 6:34 inscribed beside her. It was magnificent, and I had to fight back tears. We invited them in our home and showed them Kelsey's bedroom. Today the cross stands at the accident site along with a smaller cross put up by classmate Bailey Campbell and former Lubbock-Cooper student Jessica Crumpler.

For years, I had driven passed roadside crosses marking the accidents of Kelsi Cook and Andrea Rodriguez. At the time, I imagined how terrible it must be for the parents to drive by the site of where their child was killed. Did they avoid the place? Take a different route? Now I was faced with the same dilemma.

Despite drugs, I still could not sleep for more than a few hours. At 1:30 a.m., Monday morning, I pushed myself from bed, pulled on yesterday's clothes, and drove to the gravesite. I sat down and cried as my mind ran to the accident. I tried to imagine what the twins had seen as the dump truck bore down on them. I realized that Kayla would have this vision for the rest of her life. She had witnessed her twin being killed. Would she have survivor's guilt? We would have to watch for that. I imagined Kelsey's grief if Kayla had been the one to die. Kayla was like me: she kept things inside. Not Kelsey. If she had been the survivor, her grief would have been overt and palpable. I wondered again if Kelsey had what is called an out-of-body experience. Who greeted Kelsey upon arrival in heaven? Would Kelsey be there when I arrived? Would I arrive?

I rose and went to my office about a quarter of a mile away. I put on a pot of coffee and worked at my desk. My daughter may have died, but construction projects rolled on, and they had to be monitored. I had trouble concentrating on the pile on my desk, but in between bouts of crying, I forced myself to cut into the back log of mail, e-mail and faxes.

The administration office staff arrived at 8:00 a.m., and I did not want to have to talk to anyone, so I went home. I sat on Kelsey's bed and peered up at Proverbs 3:5. Just what does it mean to trust? I remembered the second part of the verse: "Do not lean on your own understanding." That meant rely on God. But God had let Kelsey die. Why? Why, when she had so much more to offer as a witness for Christ? It made no sense. I looked at a photograph on her desk of John Michael and her that I took of them on her 18th birthday. It always reminded me of the song by the Carpenters, "We've Only Just Begun.[9]" Now I looked at it, and anger swelled inside me at the sense of their loss. Why!? I slammed my fist on her desk next to the photograph knocking it over.

What I did not know at the time was that I had not been the only one to make night visits to the gravesite. Indeed, John Michael had spent all or part of the previous three nights out there with either his father or his friends, Austin Taylor and Brian Valigura. "We would pray, worship and seek the Lord's heart," JM wrote me later. "I still had no idea what God was doing, and why all these things had to happen to make me who I needed to be." And yet, he firmly believed that was what was precisely occurring. Then in the back of his mind a thought: what if growth was first a tearing down, instead of a building up? Like weight lifting.

On the third night, Monday, September 8, Austin and Brian joined JM. The day had been warm and sunny, and now the stars were out. They worshipped, while using Austin's car stereo for Christian music. At one point, while JM stood over the grave alone, the song "I Will Rise" by Chris Tomlin came over the radio[10]. JM started praying out loud. "God, if You are going through the valley with me, if You are going to use this horrible event that is yet absolutely part of Your plan, then make it rain. Show me Father that You are going through it with me." He raised his hands up and asked God to bring rain. "Even if it's just one drop." Then he told Kelsey he loved her, and they left.

All the way home John Michael watched for a raindrop to fall on the windshield. Nothing. Then as he was walking into his home, Austin yelled, "JM!" He turned around and Austin pointed. A few rain drops splattered the sidewalk. Then a few more. And within a few minutes, it was pouring. He grabbed a Styrofoam cup, and placed a rock in it and set it outside. "Lord, You have brought this rain. Let this cup be me, and the rain be You. Overflow this cup, and show me what You will do in my life."

The next morning, JM checked the cup. It had, indeed, overflowed.

By the time I returned home from the office on Monday morning, Jeremy had returned to work for the first time since the accident. Although he had a hard time concentrating and spent much of the day in a daze, he fought his way through the work day, several times having to find a private spot to cry. By now a sense of guilt was creeping into his consciousness. "I should have been there for her more often," he told me. I told him the six year age difference made that difficult. He did not want to hear my rationalizations.

Tuesday morning, with the help of drugs, I was able to sleep a little longer and was not in the office until 5:00 a.m. Later, we took Kayla to a specialist for her ankle and she was fitted with a boot. She did not complain about the pain, but I could tell it still hurt. Furthermore, I could tell by the way she asked questions that she was worried about permanent damage and the loss of her senior year of basketball.

Sometime later that day, Alexandra Nanny gave Kayla a six-inch by four-inch flat rock. Glued to it was Matthew 6:34 and a photograph of Paige Sterling, Alexandra and the twins. Alexandra left a note that she was going to be Kayla's rock. Kayla placed the rock in her basketball locker and kept it there all school year. That evening we went to the Lubbock-Cooper volleyball game to show our support of the girls. It had been one week since the accident, and I think many people were pleasantly surprised that we got out. It was a symbol that we were not going to give up.

About this time, our insurance agent and family friend, Trina Ehlers, said something to me that at the time I did not appreciate. She said, "Be glad that Kelsey was doing everything she was supposed to do." Her seat belt was fastened, she was not on the cell phone, and she had been paying attention. At first, I thought she was saying this from a legal perspective, but as time went on, I understood why that fact was important.

Wednesday, Bec returned to her first grade class at school. It felt good to do "something normal," even though the day was far from normal. The other grade teachers kept a close eye on her. Just in case.

Kayla went back to school on Wednesday, too. I opened doors and carried her books for her. As we came through the door, she was mobbed. People rushed to her, and it took her about ten minutes to get to her locker and then to her first class. I checked on her several times during the day to make sure she was doing okay. She always gave me a thumbs-up. However, she said it was all very awkward. "Everyone stared at me. I felt on display." She added that everyone was very supportive, "but some of the questions got a little weird. They wanted to know details about the accident. Whose fault was it? I didn't want to talk about the accident. One person even asked, 'What would you say if you could talk to Kelsey one last time?'" It was a little too fast, too personal.

During that day, Kayla started rehab on her ankle with school trainer, Sara Cayton. After school, we stopped by the gravesite. Kayla stared at the grave and then looked up at me with a pained, hollow look that seemed to say: what are we supposed to do when we are here?

I shrugged at her, and she frowned a reply. We did not stay long.

Likewise, John Michael was finding it hard to be with people for he feared they would want to talk about the accident, which was the last thing he wanted to do. It hurt too much. All he wanted to talk about was Kelsey Renee and what Christ meant to her. That was all that mattered any more.

On Wednesday, September 10, Cathy Wright, our receptionist in Central Office, told me a story about September 2. Kelsey was very close with her daughter, Raelan, a junior on the basketball team. On September 2, Kelsey and Raelan had been in the gym after shooting drills. Raelan wrote on a sheet of paper that she loved Kelsey and Kayla, as well as Ashley Parr and Bethany Boyd, both juniors on the team. "Who else do you love?" Kelsey asked. "I don't know," Raelan answered. "Why, you love Jesus," Kelsey said, so Raelan wrote on the paper, "I love Jesus!" Kelsey wrote in the corner how amazing Raelan was and how much she loved her. Raelan kept the paper, and she and Kelsey skipped to their cars arm-in-arm. Five minutes later Kelsey was dead.

Cathy gave me the now laminated sheet of paper with two photographs of Raelan and Kelsey together, and then told me the story about the rain on September 2. As I remembered the day, September 2 was a mostly sunny day. However, Raelan said that right after the accident it sprinkled for about two minutes. Kelsey loved rain.

Over twenty months after the accident, Rick Saldana, now Lubbock-Cooper's Director of Safety & Emergency Management, told me a similar story. On September 2, 2008, then Lieutenant Rick Saldana was the first law enforcement officer on the scene. He got out of his squad car and began walking towards the accident scene. As he approached, he felt a cold mist flush over him, like passing through a veil of some sort. A chill spread through his entire body.

Again, September 2 was mostly a sunny day. Was the sudden rain and the strange mist God's tears? Or just a coincidence?

After the accident, my sister and I decided to not tell my mom. Her stroke had left her unable to speak, and Kathy and I felt that telling mother about Kelsey served no purpose. It would fill her with emotions that she could not adequately express. However, word of the accident spread through the churches of my hometown, and some visitor to mom's room in her long-term assisted care unit told mom about the accident, although they had got it wrong and said "grandson." Kathy had to tell mom. That Wednesday night, I called mom to reassure her that we were doing all right. It was a difficult call to make, and I doubt it did much to soothe my mother.

On Thursday, September 11, I met for the first time with an attorney named Nolan Greak. Again, Bec had wanted me to do this before the funeral. I could hear an underlining rage in the low, growl of her voice. I could see her anger in the tension of her set jaw and the dead-on focus of her eyes. Becky was by nature sweet and tender, an easy going, easy forgiving type of personality and soul. She had to be, to put up with me all these decades. But they had killed her daughter, her best friend. And now they would pay.

I had chosen Nolan at the suggestion of Allen Adkins, another attorney who served on the Lubbock-Cooper Board of Trustees. I told Allen we wanted someone ethical, not some ambulance chaser. Allen sent me to Nolan, and it was excellent advice.

We sought a lawyer based on preliminary reports that the dump truck owned and operated by Armor Asphalt, Inc. of Lubbock had defective brakes and steering. A subsequent report by the Texas Department of Public Safety (DPS, the state highway patrol) confirmed these facts. Furthermore, we had been told that a local television had aired an interview with an eyewitness that said they had seen the Armor dump truck weaving in traffic. However, later we learned that the eyewitness had given a false name and could not be traced. To an A-J web article, someone had commented that this company had "done this kind of thing before." We were told that the steering wheel of the dump truck had over twenty inches of free play in it before it engaged. We received letters from other attorneys describing the case as one of "gross negligence."

We also learned from the DPS report that the dump truck weighed 40,000 pounds, was nearly 30 years old, and had been traveling over 50 miles per hour as it approached the intersection where the driver, Pedro Alcorte, (nearly age 70) allegedly was supposed to have turned: an elderly man at the end of a working day driving a twenty ton vehicle with faulty brakes and steering going too fast to turn onto a narrow residential street veered into the other lane and snuffed out the life of one daughter, and endangered the life of the other, leaving her physically harmed and emotionally scarred. I admit that I harbored some revenge fantasies.

Then the rains came. Over the next day or two, twelve inches of rain pounded the usually dry South Plains. I remember thinking that I did not like the idea of rain beating down on Kelsey's grave. Admittedly, not a rational response.

Towards the end of the first week after the funeral, Kayla finally spoke of the accident. We listened without interrupting, knowing that she had to get this out, and we had to hear it. "We turned off Woodrow Road onto Indiana Avenue. I was looking down texting Todd. All of the sudden, Kelsey yelled, 'Oh, no!' My head jerked up, and I saw a giant dump truck veering into our lane heading straight for us. Kelsey hit the brakes and swerved to the right, but it was too late... Everything went dark. I remember opening my eyes and the air was filled with dust. The air bag had deployed. The car was crushed in on us. The windshield was only inches from my face. Glass was shattered everywhere. I remember before I reached for the door handle, I turned and quickly looked at Kelsey. She wasn't moving, and there was a lot of blood."

Kayla thought she remembered getting out of the car on her own. However, later DPS informed us they had to cut her seat belt to get her out.

"Once I was out of the car, I fell to my hands and knees, and I could feel someone standing over me, but I did not look up. I managed to get to my feet, and I then turned around to try and get Kelsey out of the car. I screamed her name several times, but she never answered. I buried my face into my hands and started crying uncontrollably. Someone walked me to a truck and sat me down on the tailgate. I looked up and standing next to me was Mrs. Cooper. I was a bit relieved to see someone I knew. She asked me for my dad's cell phone number, but I was in such shock and could not remember it. I hugged her and asked where the ambulance was so that they could help Kelsey. The ambulance did finally arrive, and that's when you ran up as they were loading me onto the stretcher. I could hear you crying and yelling and moaning. It was horrible."

"The ride in the ambulance was terrible. I couldn't understand why they took me away first and not Kelsey. Kelsey was in worse shape than me. I kept asking the EMT guys how Kelsey was, and all they would tell me was that, 'They had people back there working on her.' I knew they were lying. I could see it in their faces. At that moment I prayed, 'Lord, I do not care if both of my feet are broken, and I can never walk again. I just want Kelsey to be okay!' ...Of course, she wasn't okay."

It was the only time she voluntarily spoke of the accident to us. I made a mental note that in a few weeks, after her physical wounds had healed, I would talk to her about counseling. And then told myself: maybe it would need to be family counseling.

Friday, September 12, we did not have school because of the flooding caused by the rain. However, in Texas, football goes on, and that evening we traveled to Muleshoe where it had not rained as much. The Lubbock-Cooper football team had put "15" decals on their helmets (Kelsey's basketball number), Kayla's name on the back of the helmet, an intricate patch on their jerseys, the design of which was made into a special flag. On one side of the flag was a large "15," and on the other side was the design of the jersey patch: "Vines" at the top, "15" in the background and a white cross with "9-2-08" on it. Senior captain, Tyler Sutton, a pallbearer and close friend of Kelsey, led the team onto the field hoisting the flag above him, then the team huddled around the flag and prayed. I grabbed Bec, and I was so choked up I could not speak for several minutes. We sat in the stands crying and holding each other, while Tyler planted the flag in the ground on the sideline. Later, I put one of the jersey patches on my Lubbock-Cooper administration jacket.

This book is first and foremost a testament to God, but after that it is homage to Lubbock-Cooper. September was a time of shock and awe. The shock is obvious. The awe was at the support we received from the Lubbock-Cooper community.

Amanda Kitten, senior classmate, wrote a wonderful letter and then a subsequent essay published in the A-J. Her mother, Jane, organized a scholarship in Kelsey's name, which we now award every May to two LCHS seniors. Senior classmate, Kandace Bowie, wrote a lovely poem. Another classmate, Morgan Abbott, wrote another very personal poem, along with a DVD that contained memories of their time together.

Friends left letters at the gravesite. Hayden Homen wrote a blog that had such spiritual insight; it was more typical of a sophomore in seminary, rather than high school. Austin Huskey, a Lubbock-Cooper baseball player wrote us describing how during a game when Kelsey was taking photographs from the dug-out, he had complained to her about not getting to play. Kelsey replied, "But then you wouldn't be here talking to me," and giggled. He chuckled and cheered up. "Your daughter," he wrote, "had a way of making people laugh in the worst of times." Then he asked if it was okay to put her name and Matthew 6:34 on his stock race car. I wrote him back that we would be honored. Another Lubbock-Cooper

63

senior, George De La Cruz, likewise put Kelsey's name and a Bible verse on his stock car.

A boy basketball player, Alex Jaskoviak, had a special sticker made displaying a pirate flag that said "In memory of Kelsey, 15." I have one on the back window of my car, as do Becky and Kayla, and many others. I still see that sticker on the back window of many cars at school, and it always brings a smile to my face.

For weeks we received a dozen letters and cards each day. They came from Lubbock-Cooper people, others area schools, the Lubbock community and the surrounding counties, ex-students from other schools at which we had taught, friends from across Texas and the nation, and complete strangers. We even received a letter from a man in jail who had read the story and was motivated to turn his life around.

During this time, it seemed like a daily affair that we were told of someone who had been impacted by Kelsey's story: there was a young girl who decided to be baptized after hearing of Kelsey's faith; a couple who was headed for divorce decided to give it another try after reading about Kelsey; kids exhorting their parents to go to church; others buying Bibles or placing them with Gideon's. I was in awe of the impact of my own daughter, and it made me miss her that much more. I wanted her to be there so I could tell her of the good she had done, of the pride I felt for her. It was all horribly bittersweet, indeed.

Sometime during the week after the funeral, Bethany Boyd told us how during the first week of school, Kelsey had pulled her aside and told her she had a feeling that the Lord was going to do "something amazing" that would bring Lubbock-Cooper High School together. Now it seemed that the event was Kelsey's death. Based on this story, and the story around Matthew 6:34, people have suggested that Kelsey knew the accident was coming. I don't know the answer. Maybe God was preparing her subconsciously. It's possible.

All of these acts, of course, did not remove the pain of losing Kelsey, but they did let us know that Kelsey was loved and remembered, and we were loved and supported. Lubbock-Cooper really is a very special place, and West Texans are the best people I know.

Was there some inappropriate comments? Of course. "You'll get over it." "It's all part of God's plan." As if God needed defending. "Just be glad for the time you had with her." "God needed another angel." So forth. Cliches. Sometimes something beyond clichés. We never really got mad at these comments. After all, these people were just trying to be helpful and did not know what to say. I had been where they were.

I did know that Kelsey's death touched a nerve. There was anger and outrage at a wrongful death. There was fear. A dump truck simply swerves into your lane. How do prevent that? There was honor and awe: she was a genuine Christian, the real deal. People admire authenticity.

And there was some guilt. Because she was gullible and good-natured, Kelsey had been frequently teased. She could say things or ask questions that would make you stop and turn towards her with a look of incredulity. I sensed after the accident that some people were experiencing a degree of guilt over having kidded Kelsey.

And so was I. Feeling guilty, that is. But for a different reason. I was supposed to protect my family, and I had not. Freak accident or not, I felt I should have trained them for that situation. That's what fathers do. They protect their daughters. And I didn't. Over time, I saw that I was not being entirely rational. But not in September 2008. Emotions are not rational. Grief is not rational. Love is not rational.

September 2008: Sadness, shock, fear, anger, awe, confusion and guilt - a powerful emotional cocktail running through me like an alternating current.

On Saturday, September 13, a mere eleven days after the accident, we purchased a new car for Kayla. I was not ready for her to be driving again, and part of me was glad that she would not be driving for several more weeks until the boot was taken off her right ankle. Frankly, I dreaded the day she would be out on the road again, but I knew that day had to come. It was part of the healing process, part of going on. As I said to someone, "What am I supposed to do? Be her chauffer for the rest of her life?"

On Sunday we attended Indiana Avenue Baptist Church, where the funeral had taken place. I felt a degree of consternation as we walked in, for I was not a fundamentalist and still harbored significant doubts about Biblical inerrancy and putting trust in the

Lord. However, we were warmly greeted at IABC, and despite my doubts, I knew I wanted to return and search for answers.

Jeremy started attending Trinity Church with Shannon Henderson. He asked if we objected if he went to a different church, and I said, "No, just as long as you go somewhere." We had Jeremy over for supper several nights a week to keep an eye on him. Jeremy tended to keep things inside. He said he missed Kelsey, but otherwise was doing all right. I could see he was torn up inside like the rest of us, and he admitted he was still having trouble concentrating on his college classes.

I remember praying during the month of September mostly for protection for my family: please, God, do not let this happen again to anyone in my family; while a little voice in the back of my mind said: but you prayed for that before. Fear was fueling my thoughts towards God. I wanted a guarantee. Is hope different from trust, or is it two sides of the same coin?

For all of us, evenings became a tough time. During the day, our jobs and classes occupied just enough of our consciousness that we could usually keep the demons at bay. But at night, they had their way with us, sweeping into the void, rolling over us, consuming us.

It hit Becky just as soon as she left the school parking lot. By the time she reached home, her mood had been captured and altered, and that pervasive sick feeling dogging her day morphed into anger and bitterness. Sometimes Becky took it out on the house, attacking house work with a gritty anger. The vacuum cleaner clawed. The mop beat. The duster whacked. Over the entire house, she rolled. Except Kelsey's room. That went untouched. And when the fury finally faded, she would walk into Kelsey's room and a feeling of peace would set in. I could not go in there without crying or wreathing, but it spread God's soothing balm on Becky.

Kelsey's absence in the house at night was so thick that at times it seemed like a ghost in itself. It altered sleeping patterns. Becky could sleep, with enough drugs, while I could not sleep more than a few hours at a time even with drugs. Jeremy found escape by sleeping more than ever, while Kayla kept reliving the accident over and over seeing the dump truck bear down on them. She would cry herself to sleep, and just before she would slip off, she would ask: God, why was I spared? Months later, I learned that JM still could not sleep in his room, finding whatever slumber he could manage in the back guest room. Indeed, it was not until July 2009, that he could finally return to his bed.

Mornings provided a special challenge for Kayla. As she got ready at her sink and mirror, she would glance to her right, and there, standing like sentries on guard duty, was Kelsey's stuff just as she had left them on the morning of September 2. It was like they were at attention, waiting for her to return. Kayla would finish getting ready and then drive to school. Alone.

For John Michael, mornings were about a thundering silence: no wake-up call or text from his sweety. No making plans for the evening. Just another day without Kelsey Renee.

For me, the longing and heartache at this time was relentless, manifesting in a heaviness in my chest and a sick feeling in my stomach. Once a day I had a good cry just to relieve the pressure that built up inside of me. I also noticed that pangs of grief made Kels feel nearer. Sometimes it seemed like she was right beside me giving me a hug trying to comfort me. I remember reading once that grief can become its own kind of drug. Now I could understand why.

I think it was during the second week after the funeral that we received three beautiful pencil drawings of Kelsey. Her hair was made up of expressions and verses. It was stunning. Someone named "John" drew the three pieces. We never knew more than that.

On Monday, September 15, there was a Letter to the Editor in the A-J speculating that all the rain we were getting was because of losing Kelsey. I remember thinking: is this how public this has become?

On Friday we had a home football game against Idalou, and their student council presented Kayla at mid-field before the game with a check for over $1,000 for the Kelsey Vines Memorial Scholarship. Many other surrounding schools sent cards and money, as well. We did not solicit or advertise. It was a spontaneous gesture for everyone, and we were deeply touched. Furthermore, it fed a growing need. If we could somehow do some good, like a scholarship, then the sting of Kelsey's death was diminished, at least, a little.

On Saturday we met with Paula Sadler of Sadler Monuments

to pick a grave marker. She was very helpful and caring. Later, she contributed a beautiful granite bench to the memorial garden Kayla built for Kelsey.

"Firsts" started playing a part in our lives. I remember the first time I filled my car with gasoline. I felt guilty, as if I was betraying Kelsey by doing the mundane things and going on with my life. A Lubbock-Cooper student, Riley Howell, was working at the store and saw me leaning against the pump with my head down. He said over the intercom, "God bless you, Mr. Vines." I wished him the same. It made me feel better. Little things like that mattered more than ever. Kind words are rarely wasted. Two years later, his younger brother, Nathan, took his freshman school photograph wearing his "Kelsey" shirt.

Another "first" was laughing again. Initially, when I would hear someone laughing in the office or some other place, I felt a jab of anger. How dare you be enjoying yourself!? I always stopped myself from saying anything, but I thought it. When I finally laughed myself, I felt guilty. What's the matter with me? I asked. I shouldn't be laughing. It took me several more weeks to laugh without being consumed by guilt. However, even now sometimes a patina of guilt creeps in when I laugh or experience joy. Jeremy said he had the same feeling.

In September, grief colored everything. Someone would mention something in 1988, and I would say to myself: oh, that was before we knew we would lose a child. Several books arrived in the mail, though I did not feel like reading anything yet. I got calls from people whom I had not talked to in years.

Every night the house continued to be filled with people. Most said things like, "I can't imagine what you're going through," "You're inspiring us," or "You're the strongest people I know." I wanted to say, "Is that how it looks?" Pam Brown, the Director of Guidance for Lubbock-Cooper, told me, "You taught all of us how to grieve." I think I gave her a blank stare, because I had no idea to what she was alluding. We were just trying to get through each day.

The level of support we received was incredible, and the key people day-in and day-out were Pat and Jo, Kyle Edwards and his family, and John Michael. No matter how bad I was feeling, as soon as JM walked through the door, I instantly felt better. Here was someone suffering as much as we were, and yet his faith was undeterred. He gave me hope.

At this point, I visited the gravesite nearly every day and "talked" to Kels. I always told her how much I loved her and how much she was missed by everyone. I also told her how much I admired her for her witness for Christ and apologized for not saying that to her when she was alive. I regretted that I had not told her when I had the chance, and I resolved that when I saw her in heaven that would be the first thing I would say to her.

It was about this time that I began to ask "what if?" What if Kelsey had swerved just a bit earlier? Why didn't I train them for just this scenario? I felt myself getting mad at her and then at myself. What if Kayla had been driving? Would she have swerved earlier? What if the road had been a few feet wider; what if they had obeyed me and not driven down narrow, pot-hole filled Woodrow Road? What if the timing had been a second different: if the dump truck had been one second earlier or later, or if the Grand Am had been one second earlier or later?... each vehicle had been going in the low 50 miles per hour range, which meant each vehicle was traveling over 70 feet a second. One mere second, one fraction of a second. Becky wondered what if we had not retained them in the second grade. Then they would be in college now and probably not on that road at that time. What if we had stayed in Mart, and not moved back to Lubbock? What if? What if? It made us miserable.

Then other "what ifs" started to creep into our consciousness. What if Kayla had been the one to die? How would Kelsey have dealt with it? What if both of them had died!? What if we had any doubt about Kelsey being in heaven? I understood now what Trina had said to me: what a blessing that Kelsey had been doing everything she was supposed to have done. The "what ifs" would have been a lot worse.

However, the "what ifs" did serve one useful purpose. It worked through my mind something like this: when Kelsey saw the dump truck veering towards her, she froze. Why!? I don't know, but she did. She could have jerked the steering wheel to the right and sped into the ditch. *Why didn't she?* She could have slammed on the brakes. *Why didn't she?* She could have gunned the accelerator. She could have even turned hard to the left, and the dump truck might have sliced in front of her, and maybe missed the car. *Why didn't she?* Any of those things might have changed the outcome - possibly for the better (but also possibly for the worse). What if she had done this? What if she had done that? What if? Over and over, I asked this. A dozen possible scenarios. Finally, I said enough. And a fact formed in my mind. Somehow, what had happened was God's plan, and I had to accept it. I did not know why it was God's way, but it was. I did not know how it fit His purpose, but it did. And on that day a kernel of trust began to germinate- still delicate and fragile, but growing nonetheless.

I also noticed about this time that when I was driving and would see another dump truck or large vehicle, I would wince, slow down and move to my right. And as I did, I pictured what the dump truck must have looked like bearing down on them. Then I would remind myself that Kayla did not have to imagine this. All she had to do was remember it, which she would do for the rest of her life. Several times I wanted to storm into the dump truck company or pound on the home door of the driver. Do you know what you have done!? Do you see how many lives you have devastated!?

Bitterness began to creep into me, and I had to struggle to resist it. I would think of people who had not visited, called, or sent a letter, and resented them. Then I would remind myself: I did not always write or call when others were in similar circumstance. Why not? Because I did not know what to say. And these people now did not know what to say to us. Someone would start giving me advice on how to deal with grief, and I would have to resist snapping: Oh? How do you know? You've never gone through this.

Meanwhile, I continued to watch for any sign of survivor's guilt in Kayla, particularly after she asked me: "How come Kelsey was killed and so little injury was done to me?" I questioned her and concluded she did not blame herself for still being alive. She blamed Armor Asphalt and the driver, Pedro Alcorte.

These feelings of sadness, bitterness, anger, regret, guilt, fear, pride and awe were not linear. They did not come in some pre-packaged sequence; rather, they flipped through my mind like the turning of a kaleidoscope. They would come and go with an alarming speed and would gyrate from positive to negative and back again, like a ping pong match. Each day was different. Each hour and sometimes even each minute was different. It was hard to stay on a stable course when we were being twisted and thrown around so much.

On Tuesday, September 23, the Middle School band, directed by Dale Stelzer played a special rendition of "Holy, Holy, Holy" for Kelsey. It was very moving. That Saturday, Pat, Jo and Lanny and Vicky Lincecum came over. We were watching football and enjoying each other's company. A wave of grief swept over me. Here I was watching football as if nothing had happened. I went into Kelsey's room, found her basketball jersey, laid down on her bed, draped the jersey over my chest, and closed my eyes. The next thing I knew, Becky was at my side crying and trying to comfort me.

Sunday the 28th was the first night since the accident that there were no visitors. It felt odd.

Sometime during the month of September, I received my passport. I had applied for it in August, and sometime during the later part of September it arrived in the mail. The date of issue: September 2. I remember staring at the date, noting the bitter irony, and wondering if it did not somehow symbolize a passing and a port: the passing of my daughter and of that reality through a port into some new reality, a reality that still did not seem real. A reality without an apparent path. A reality without a clear destination. It seemed to capture the confusion of September.

There was one other emotion I want to mention. I was barely aware of it at the time. It was like a fish swimming ten feet below the water line. It darted here and there, and I caught only glimpses and shadows. It was joy. Every once in a while I peered through the pain and thought of Kelsey in heaven. She had made it. She was happy- happier than any human on earth; happier than I had ever dreamed of being. This feeling of joy was only a flicker piercing the pain of September, but it was there. And it would grow.

Chapter Eight
October

Hard Grief Sets In

"The Lord will guide you continually, and satisfy
your soul in drought, and strengthen your bones;
you shall be like a watered garden, and like a
spring of water, whose waters do not fail."
Isaiah 58:11

During September we marked each Tuesday. One week, two weeks... Starting in October we started noting the second day of the month. One month. What would the second one bring?

The answer came almost immediately: hard grief. Shock ruled September, numbing us to reality. In October the anesthetic wore off. Kelsey is gone. That's the way it is. Deal with it.

Every Tuesday, John Michael still received dozens of texts expressing condolences and prayers. Each one served to remind him how much Kelsey was loved and he was loved, and yet each one was its own reminder that Kelsey was gone. In the month of October, hard reality bore in, and for all of us, October was in some ways more painful than September.

A pervasive sadness set in that was like someone standing behind me pressing down on my shoulders. I had never been in anything that consumed me as much as this. There were literally very few waking minutes that I did not think about it for at least a second or two in some capacity. The anger I felt at this time was watching my loved ones deal with their sadness and knowing I could not take it away. Sometimes Becky was in so much agony that she would sit in her chair in the living room and squeeze her eyes closed, as if she could not see the world, then she would not have to feel it. I felt helpless, and that frustrated me to the point of anger.

Bec, on the other hand, was beyond anger. She was bitter. She wanted the potential law suit against Armor Asphalt to proceed much faster. "They just can't kill someone and not suffer any consequences. These people have got to be stopped." We were waiting on further investigations by DPS. We did not know at this time that it would take many more months before the Motor Carrier Report was complete.

Pressure continued to build up, and everyday, or at least every few days, I would need a good cry to spill the tension. In the past, I had an ulcer caused by acid reflux. Under the stress of grief, the ulcer returned, exacerbated by the fact I started drinking more. Emotions oscillated: bouts of anger swung to spurts of joy as I thought of Kelsey in heaven; bitterness gyrated to gratitude towards those who had helped us; confusion over why God would let this happen arched into the conviction that God *must* have some reason for this (but what!?); and, despair gave way to the hope of seeing Kelsey again someday. Grief, I discovered, was an ever-changing cornucopia of positives and negatives.

One moment I would be just fine, and the next grief could blind-side me, hitting me when I did not expect it. A name, a sound, even a smell could trigger some memory, and wham it would hit me like a kidney shot. It could come with a mesmerizing speed, and suddenly I found myself crying, even wailing. Good days were followed by crushing ones. Grief was sneaky.

I also learned that grief was exhausting: emotionally and physically. I had been going for weeks on adrenaline and a few hours of drug-induced poor sleep. At times I would sit in the chair at home, and my body felt as if it was humming like a car at idle. I knew I could not keep going like this.

At certain times it seemed like months since Kels had died, and at other times it felt like just a few hours ago. Nights were still the worst time. I missed her giggles. I missed her goofy jokes. I even missed her moods. Loneliness and anger. What if? Why!? Lots of demons. John Michael was over one night, and I heard him tell Becky, "If Kels was here I'd say 'let's get married right now.'" I thought of leading her down the aisle and smiled, then it snapped into a frown. I'll never get to do that, and I slammed my fist on the kitchen counter. People kept telling us how strong we were. Boy, I thought, do we have them fooled.

We didn't have Ronnie Quest fooled. Ronnie Quest, the former board member who had lost a daughter, stopped by my office. He sat down in one of my chairs, looked straight at me, and asked, "How you doing?"

"I'm okay," I answered.

"You're a liar."

I resolved right there to quit lying to everyone, and particularly myself, that I was doing okay. I was not doing okay. From here on out, when someone asked how I was doing, I would not give the perfunctory "Good." I was not going to mope, but I would not lie, either.

Ronnie went on to tell me how grief still worked on him and his family. "It's not going to get much better," he said.

I did not believe him. It's *got* to get better, I told myself. We can't stay this way the rest of our lives.

"The only question is whether you have a teary moment or a complete meltdown," he continued.

Likewise, JM had come to a similar conclusion. He was not good, and he was not going to say he was when he wasn't. And echoing at the back of his mind the question: will I ever be "good" again?

About that time we received a letter from Debbie Sharp, a friend from our days in Mart. They had lost a son in a car accident more than a decade ago. "I wish I could tell you it gets easier, but it doesn't," she wrote. Another person wrote warning us that our lives had been ruined forever. I remember thinking at the time these people have got to be wrong, but a little voice said: hey, they've been there.

I remembered a conversation with then high school principal, Berta Fogerson, now Lubbock-Cooper's Assistant Superintendent. Years ago, her brother had drowned. Berta told me how her mom said there was always a hole in her life after that. A hole: that was a good way to describe how I felt. A massive, gaping sink hole in our lives. People would say "I can't imagine what you're going through," and I would reply, "If you have kids you can imagine it, but it's worse than that."

In its own way grief also became a kind of sick companion because it kept me in touch with Kelsey. When I cried and ached, I felt closer to Kelsey, and I discovered that I needed those crying times not just as a release, but as a way to draw her near to me. There is a certain addictive quality to grief.

We had been given several books on grief, but I could not yet read them for I feared what they would say about the future; that, indeed, the worst was yet to come. I was flipping through one, *Don't Take My Grief Away From Me* by Doug Manning, and saw the title chapter, "Please Don't Take My Grief Away From Me.[11]" The title intrigued me, and I read that particular chapter. It rung true. Until one goes through a severe loss, one cannot understand the truth of how at times one clings to grief as something real amidst the surreal nature of tragedy.

However, reality was never far away. I would hear about a car accident, and I would cringe as I imagined what that family was going through and what was before them. I went to a high school volleyball game and saw two young twins playing together, and it brought back memories of Kayla and Kelsey. Each morning I experienced a bittersweet sensation when I turned on my cell phone. Kels had placed on it a message: "Good morning, dad. Have a good day. Kels, :) ."

For Becky and Kayla, mornings, too, continued to be a special challenge as they got ready. For Becky, it was what was there: sitting on the vanity was a photograph of Kels and her together at Myrtle Beach. It was like Kelsey was sitting there watching her put on her make-up. For Kayla, it was what was not there: the open space at the sink where Kelsey was supposed to be standing.

What did make me feel better was the idea of doing something good: awarding a scholarship, answering the many letters, helping others with similar grief. Somehow the grief was more manageable and made more sense if I could make some good out of the tragedy. I guess that's why I had to write this book despite the pain of reliving it.

We continued to have Jeremy over for supper several times a

week to check his pulse. He seemed to be doing a little better. He said he could concentrate better on his classes, but you could tell Kelsey's loss hung on him like it did us.

Kayla was still crying herself to sleep at night and having an occasional nightmare. She was like me. She kept things inside. I continued to watch for survivor's guilt, but when I would question her, she always directed any blame towards Armor Asphalt and the driver. I asked her why God had spared her. For what purpose? She shrugged, but I could see that the question had been weighing on her mind.

Meanwhile, a modicum of guilt began festering inside me. During the month of October, it became apparent that we would probably be getting some insurance money, maybe even enough to pay off our mortgage. And while we knew no amount of money was going to even the ledger, the fact we would gain at all from the tragedy at first seemed perverted to me.

Becky was exactly the opposite. She wanted punitive damages. The more the better. She wanted Armor Asphalt out of business and owner Jimmy Hogan and driver Pedro Alcorte in jail. When I told her none of those things were likely to happen, she turned towards me and said through gritted teeth: "Well, they should happen."

Music demonstrated a divide, became a road marker. I would hear a favorite song and remember how it used to make me feel before Kelsey died. Particular memories were associated with respective songs. Now all they did was serve to remind me of my life before September 2.

For Becky, an almost robotic monotony set in during October. "As I look back on it," she told me later, "in some ways I shut down. I was simply going through the motions. And everyday, as I turned onto 98th Street to come home, it hit me that Kelsey would not be there when I got home. The way I dealt with that was to go numb."

The stress and apathy led to some temporary weight gain. After losing pounds during the initial shock in September, she filled some of the void in October by eating. Always a stress eater, she remarked later, "It's a wonder I did not gain a hundred pounds that year."

I went numb, too, but in a different way. Festering inside of me like a cancer, was a growing apathy, and it surprised me. That was not me. But it had become me. I still could not ride my bike or exercise. It was too life-affirming. Furthermore, I would watch the news and shrug: so what? I had been a political science major and a government teacher. This detachment towards current events I was now feeling was not the usual me.

I would watch men postulate. I would observe women predicate. I saw striving and heard yearning all about me. And I did not feel part of any of it. I was outside looking in on a throbbing world, a foreigner in my own life.

The apathy manifested first as distraction: I found I could not concentrate at work for more than an hour or two before I would push the papers from me. At first I thought I was just tired, which I most certainly was. But gradually, I recognized that I did not care about work as much as I usually did. I had always been passionate about my career in education. I saw it as making a difference. But now I found myself thinking what's it matter? I knew that if I did not change this attitude, I would have to retire at the end of the 2008-09 school year.

Part of the problem was that the apathy felt good. To a significant degree, I lost my dread of dying. Death? Okay, that means I get to see Kelsey. I saw a special on the History Channel that predicted Armageddon in 2012. Fine by me. No more pain. I was already in a daily struggle not to conclude that our lives had been ruined, and death would simply be a way out. This was never suicidal in nature. Not once did I contemplate taking my life as an escape; rather, I saw death, if it came, as not the great bogey-man I had earlier in my life. Frankly, this detachment for life was rather liberating.

It also marked a distinct change in perspective. One of my favorite poems, particularly during my deistic days, was "Do Not Go Gentle Into That Good Night" by Dylan Thomas, with its famous line, "Rage, rage against the dying of the light.[12]" Life was to be seized and squeezed. It was worth fighting for, raging about.

Not any more. The only rage I felt now was towards life itself, and Jimmy Hogan, owner of Armor Asphalt, and Pedro Alcorte, the driver.

I knew I needed purpose. The only thing that gave me purpose at this point was taking care of my family. Tragedy is a test for any marriage. I had seen couples fall apart under the pressure of grief. Kels had been Bec's best friend, and I tried to fill the void in small ways, although I felt like I was failing at this. However, I must have been doing something right, for at a football game, Bunny Bednarz told me that when she asked Becky how she was doing, Bec answered, "I've got Thom." This surprised me at the time, but brought satisfaction.

In many ways, our marriage grew stronger, not weaker. It was not only a shared pain, but a mutual respect that flowered. We became like gothic buttresses leaning against each other holding each other up. When one was having a tough day, the other moved in to support the other. And we did this on instinct without cue or coaxing. Or even thanks. That was not needed. A sincere "I love you" took care of that. Moments of physical intimacy took on new power, a bittersweet immediacy. Touch and tears, we discovered, are woven into the same fabric.

October had its share of significant events. On the first, we received a nice letter from Texas Governor Rick Perry. One of his aides, John Esparza, was a former student of mine at Garden City, and he had mentioned our loss to the Governor.

The second, of course, was the first month anniversary. Had it really already been a month? Had it really been only one month?

On the 8th, Bec and I started going to classes to learn about IABC (Indiana Avenue Baptist Church). Becky had longed to go to church for a long time, and occasionally had attended with Kelsey. Going back to church reaffirmed her faith. "It's important to actually hear the word of God," she told me, "particularly in times of tragedy."

I could also see that church was bringing Kayla closer to God. "I could feel God working in my life," she told me. Jeremy kept attending Trinity with Shannon and said it was helping him, as well. As for me, church channeled my many burgeoning questions and funneled my emotions.

On one Sunday in October, Becky and I went forward towards the end of the service and knelt and prayed. Pastor McMeans knelt beside us and prayed for us. The emotional dam broke. The sadness rushed forth. The pain spilled through. Pastor McMeans put his arm around us and said, "The time of hard grief has set in."

With tears streaming down our eyes, we returned to our seats.

Johnny Vestal, JM's father, came to comfort us. I turned to him. "It should not have taken Kelsey's death to move me closer to God."

Johnny chastised me. "Whatever it takes is the way of the Lord. Accept it."

On Tuesday the 14th, I went to probate court for Kelsey's death. That evening there was a meeting of the parents of the basketball team. Kelsey's name was not on the roster, and it hurt even though we knew it would not be there.

Kayla's ankle slowly improved, although at a frustratingly slow pace. She was badly out of shape after weeks of inactivity. Practices rolled on, but Kelsey's absence was felt every time they ran a drill, every time the team huddled together. One day in October, Kayla could not take it any more. She started to cry. Coach Parsley moved to comforted her. Kayla ran to the locker room and sat at Kelsey's locker. The whole team stopped practice and rushed to Kayla. After that, Kayla realized she had to try and keep her emotions in check so that it would not effect the rest of the team. She was not always successful.

Friday, October 17 was Homecoming. Kayla had been nominated as one of the finalists for queen. At the pep rally, the five finalists were introduced, and by the applause, I knew that Kayla was the probable winner. I quickly concluded that the vote was as much a declaration about Kels as it was a statement of support for Kayla. I braced myself for the emotion of that evening. I tried to be happy about it, but just like Kelsey's name not being on the basketball roster, Kayla being queen was just another reminder that Kels was gone. The emotions swelled as I thought of the evening if Kelsey had been there. She would have been so happy for Kayla and would have been out there taking photographs as she always had. Also, there was a good chance that Kels would have been on the court herself.

As it became time to line up for the announcement, I felt myself turning hollow inside. Later, I saw photographs of me, and I could see the pain in my face. When Kayla was announced as the queen, I turned and looked at her. She put on a smile, but I could tell that she, too, was feeling the pain of Kelsey's absence. She, too, knew that this was a statement of love and support for both Kelsey and herself. As everyone swarmed around Kayla with congratulations, I tried to hold it together, but I could not. It hurt too much.

After the football game against Perryton, which we won in a late fourth quarter rally, there was the traditional dance in which King and Queen shared a dance. Bec and I watched while King Queston Evans and Kayla danced. Then we left. Afterwards, Kayla said it was the first time since the accident she enjoyed herself.

On Sunday the 19th, I watched the DVD of the funeral and realized I had not heard about two minutes of John Michael's talk. I must have been out under the valium. I listened to his speech and was awed at the power of his faith.

The next week we played our district rival, Lubbock Estacado, who had put number 15 patches on their helmets. Later, the Estacado volleyball team wore number 15 on their jerseys. Class acts by competitors, and I wrote their coaches afterwards thanking them.

Also, that week the six-foot high, white marble cross was put up by Deena Weeks. She placed it on the west side of the road. A few weeks later, someone dug up the cross, and placed it on the east side where the accident had occurred. We never knew who moved it.

Shortly after this, John Michael finally visited the accident site at Indiana and 158th. He had deliberately avoided it for weeks. He feared he would find skid marks and other haunting reminders. In fact, except for visits to the gravesite two miles east, he would never venture down Indiana or Quaker Streets further south than 110th, our street. Points south were like a no man's land, a type of forbidden zone.

Now something pulled him to go there. "I was lying on the floor crying and praying," he wrote me later. "It struck me. I have to go out there. I felt the Lord calling me out there. To meet Him out there."

It was midnight. He pushed himself from the floor and quietly slipped out of the house. He did not want to answer any questions. He wanted to do this alone. As he drove the nearly 80 blocks south down Indiana, he kept asking himself, "Am I doing the right thing? Can I handle this?" He knew he had to trust God. He turned on a Christian radio station and asked God to give him strength.

To his surprise, as he approached the accident site, he felt the burden on him easing. He parked his pick-up near the white cross and saw the photograph of Kelsey from the prom they attended last spring and the verse Matthew 6:34 next to her face. He dropped to his knees, a flood of memories rushing to him. He turned on his IPod and played some Christian songs as he prayed. As he asked why over and over, God put on his heart and mind a thought: "This is not the place where Kelsey died and was taken from us. This is the very ground where the God of this universe, the God who breathes life into each of us, caught Kelsey Renee, his daughter, into His loving arms, and now He will never let her go." A sense of peace swept over John Michael, washing his entire body with God's love. "God *is* love," he wrote me. "It is the only statement that truly matters. Everything we need branches off of His love." And there on the lonely Texas prairie, in the early hours of an October morning, John Michael wept tears of joy. For he knew he was not alone.

A few days later came October 21, the anniversary of Kelsey and his first meeting at Starbucks. All through the day, he received many calls and text messages, and yet, as he walked the sidewalks of the Texas Tech campus and passed hundreds of other students, he found himself looking at the others and thinking, "Do you have any idea what today means to me? Don't you know what I am going through?" Then he realized that all that mattered was that God knew. "We must go," he later told me, "through the valley before we can stand on top of the mountain."

It is odd that what comforts one person does not necessarily provide solace to another. For instance, there is "Kelsey's Star." In the autumn of 2008, Venus swung from being a morning star to appearing in the evening low in the southwestern sky. About this time, Jupiter could also be seen in close proximity, as could occasionally a striking crescent moon. It was quite a celestial show. Becky took to calling Venus "Kelsey's Star" for it shined brighter than the others, and I think it gave her a modicum of comfort. Not me. I would look up at the vastness of space and wonder where Heaven was. Where ever it was, it seemed like a long ways away. For me, looking at the stars made Kelsey feel more distant, not closer. Neither Bec nor I were being rational, but then grief is not always rational.

I was still not ready to read books on grief, books from a psychotherapeutic point of view. However, I was ready to read Christian books to help me sort through the spiritual questions and find some answers. For the most part, Becky resisted this route. She did not yet want to confront the pain churning inside. "I don't need a book to tell me I'm sad," she once said. However, I did get her to read Don Piper's *90 Minutes in Heaven*[13]. And her reaction stunned me.

In 1989, Baptist minister Don Piper was driving in a rural area north of Houston, Texas, when his car was struck by a semi-truck. Don Piper was pronounced dead at the scene. Ninety minutes later EMT crews found him alive. I say "found" for no medical team resuscitated him. They found him dead, and then they found him alive. During that hour and half earth time, Don Piper went to Heaven. Then he went through hell: an excruciatingly painful rehab, exacerbated by the fact that he had experienced the joy and wonder of paradise. He had seen as good as it gets. Now he was in a hospital with pain as bad as it gets. At first, he did not tell anyone about his out-of-body experience. Then over the years he began to tell his story. Finally, in 2004, at the behest of many people, he published his story.

In October 2008, I read his book and loved it. His two chapters describing his experiences in Heaven brought me great comfort. This is what Kelsey was living at this very moment. However, to my complete surprise, Becky had a completely opposite reaction. Here's why.

Again, EMT did not resuscitate Don Piper. A full ninety minutes after the accident, they checked Don's pulse again: still dead. Another Baptist minister named Dick Onerecker came upon the accident scene. He climbed into the back of what was left of Don Piper's car, prayed, and then sang for Don Piper. (There's more to the story, and I encourage you to read the book). Suddenly, Don began singing along with Onerecker, and was back alive over ninety minutes after being declared dead. Becky read this and then threw the book at my feet. I looked at her. "What's the matter?" I asked. "Didn't the book bring you a sense of peace?"

"No," she said flatly.

"Why not?"

"Why didn't God do that for Kelsey? Why didn't God bring her back?"

I was stunned. I had not considered that as a possible reaction. I had asked her to read it in the anticipation that it would bring the same sense of peace to her that it brought to me. Same star, different reactions. Same book, different reactions. Again, grief is very individual. We all react differently. And I think each person even reacts differently to different episodes of tragedy. While there *are* common denominators, each person travels the road of grief in their own way at their own pace.

Other books brought comfort, too, such as *Faith Logic: Getting Online with God* by Dr. Jim Wetherbe, a professor at Texas Tech University[14]. Jim had given a copy of his book to Dave Paschall, Lubbock-Cooper High's Associate Principal, and Dave passed it on to me. *Faith Logic* was a thought-provoking read, which used deduction as an avenue to discovering the mystic. After I finished, Jim and I met for lunch in November. Jim and his wife, Brynn, also attended my baptism, although I did not know it at the time. Later, he donated copies of his book so we could raise money for the Kelsey Vines Memorial Scholarship and Kayla's memorial garden to Kelsey.

I read the novel *The Shack* by William Young, given to me by Barry Orr, a local banker whom I had never met[15]. The first chapters were about the abduction and murder of a young girl- obviously, difficult to read. I forced myself through the early chapters in anticipation that it would be worth it. It was. Though often antithetical to Christian orthodoxy, a wonderful world of God's love spilled out from the pages. It reinforced my essential belief that Kelsey was doing quite fine. It was us that had to suffer on.

And of that I had to make sense. Since September 2 spiritual questions had pounded on me, and other than affirming that there still was a God, I had for the most part avoided seeking any answers. My main focus had been on protecting my family. However, Isaiah 45:15 aside, God made it clear that there would be no hiding from Him. He demanded my attention. As you saw in chapter three, I had traveled a twisted path to even get to the point that I believed Jesus was Christ. Now I was under direct assault again. I knew instinctively that how I answered the many questions and doubts would determine the rest of my life. Much was at stake. However, I was also resolved that this "investigation" went where ever it went. Truth was truth. I would answer the questions as honestly as I could, and chips would fall where they may.

In mid-October, I met with Pastor McMeans for over two

hours, the first of many sessions. The previous week we had started attending classes on possibly joining IABC. At this first private session, I asked Pastor McMeans some questions that had arisen during the class. We, of course, discussed my grief over Kelsey's loss. I had given him a copy of *From Ayn to Awe*, and he had waded through it, for which I was grateful. He patiently answered my many probes left over from my deist days concerning Biblical inerrancy, predestination, the working of the crucifixion, and a host of other issues, and while not all questions and doubts were answered (are they ever?), I left his office with a resolve: like it or not, I have been thrown onto a new journey, and I would make the trip. But where would it end?

After Kelsey died, I had to decide if there still was an all-powerful creator of the universe. I concluded there was. At some point, something was created out of nothing. Only a supernatural force could do that. That logical deduction was the lynch-pin, the belief that held everything else together, the rock to which that I kept returning.

The next major question confronting me: was God punishing us? Had we done something wrong? What did any of us do that would deserve this pain?

I have been assured by many people that God was not punishing us. However, cynical me concluded that some of them may have just been saying that to ease our suffering. Were we being punished? If we are being punished, I did not know what any of us did that deserved this degree of consequences. Yet, I admitted that it was possible that we were being punished. Maybe that is not the most satisfying of answers, but it is how I felt at the time.

Another early question: can this happen again? Again, there was no ready answer. It took me the rest of the year to resolve this.

What was the purpose of taking Kelsey? Why God!? Why take someone who had so much to offer as a witness for You? I kept reminding myself of the second part of Proverbs 3:5: "do not lean on your own understanding," but in October that did little to soothe the pain. I needed to know why. Things had to make sense to me. Was it because Kelsey's death could be an impetus to a spiritual awakening in my family and me? In others? In Lubbock-Cooper students? Was *she* really the "amazing something" that God was going to do in Lubbock-Cooper? Did God take her because of all of my family, she was the most ready? Is that how it works? And just why did God permit such tragedy? Why does there have to be so much heartache in this world? What is the purpose of it? Does God not want us so enamored with this world? Does God feel that if we are so attached to this life, then we will not turn to Him?

Lots of questions. Not many answers. The God of Isaiah 45: 15 truly seemed to be a God who kept Himself hidden. But why? Why not be more direct and transparent? Why leave so much hinging on faith and possible misinterpretation? I wanted to yell at the Lord: "Just tell me! And I will listen."

And questions begat more questions. A corollary of these questions concerning why was: is God "sifting" us? Is God challenging and testing us so we can grow?

Accept it? That was one thing I was not good at. Too cynical. Too stubborn. Too much pride.

To this question of purpose came a corollary query: how active was God in our lives? My deistic past resurfaced. Was the accident predestined, or were Armor and the driver to blame? Was it a human error or an act of God? Or both? Was God all-powerful? If so, why didn't He prevent it? Or was the accident part of a fallen world, and God wept, too?

Just how active was God? I used to think that God did not micro-manage our lives, but maybe I was wrong; maybe He does. For instance, was it coincidence that led Kelsey to JM, or was it God's direction? Early in 2007, Kelsey had broken up with a boy that was cheating on her, which at the time seemed like a crisis. She dated another boy for a few months, and then met JM. Coincidence, or God's loving hand?

Furthermore, we had moved from West Texas twice, and each time events coalesced to return us to the dusty plains. Coincidence, or God's plan? In my deistic past, I would have described any attempt to see that as other than coincidence as foolhardy religious superstition. But now I didn't know. One thing was clear: if God was directing all of this, then He knew when we returned to West Texas that Kelsey was going to be killed. How did that fit His purpose?

I thought on these questions at length, prayed on them, read verses on them. In 1 Corinthians 2:7 it is stated "the hidden

wisdom which God predestined." Ephesians 1:11 stated events
were "predestined according to His purpose." Acts 4:28 and
Romans 8:29 also described predetermined events. So the Bible
clearly stated that events were predestined. However, as I described
in chapter three, few things chafed me like the idea of God's plan.
I took this to mean we did not possess freedom, and if we did
not have freedom, then we really did not have responsibility. No
responsibility ran counter to my Midwestern, middle class values
of individualism.

So was Kelsey's accident predestined? Were my forebodings
of tragedy the weeks before September 2 a preparation by God?
Was Kelsey's reading of Matthew 6:34 on September 2 a similar
preparation? Is Psalm 139 true? Are our days preordained in God's
book?

I thought about this for some time and decided that certainly
God knew it was coming. Any one capable of creating something
out of nothing was not only capable of understanding the future, but
determining it, as well. If that was the case, then it *was* predestined.
A certain circular reasoning set in: If God knew the future, then
there was predestination. Then it dawned me: God *is* the future.
He is the past, and He is the future, the Alpha and Omega. He is
beyond time.

This understanding circled me right back to the question of
purpose. If God knew Kelsey would be killed on September 2,
2008, what purpose did God have in allowing that dump truck to
smash the life out of her? I was filled with questions, and I decided
I would actively seek the answers. What I did not understand at the
time was that we do not so much seek God as He seeks us.

I admit that much of my early motivation to seeking answers
was that I saw God as the avenue to see Kelsey again. Heaven
took on an immediacy that did not exist before September 2.
Heaven went from an abstract issue to one of personal yearning. I
would hear the song "There Will Be a Day" by Jeremy Camp and
imagined re-uniting with Kelsey in Heaven[16].

In this regards, John Michael was a fulcrum, leveraging our
pain, tilting us towards God. JM had made me a DVD of songs,
which introduced me to many artists, including Kim Walker. Wow!
He also showed us the video "How Great is our God" by Louie
Giglio[17]. JM told me he watched this video every night for a month

just before he went to bed, drawing from its strength. The essential theme of the video is the incredible power of God to create a universe of such mind-boggling expanse and utter complexity. Giglio described laminin, of which I had never heard. Laminin is a protein that holds together the structure of every cell. Without laminin, every cell would implode and die. Our bodies are made up of billions, maybe trillions of cells, and each relies on laminin to exist. Laminin is very much the basis of life. It's shape? A cross. Our bodies are held together by billions of crosses. The basis of life in the universe is the cross. JM insisted that it was not a coincidence.

As I watched the video, I found myself smiling broadly and deeply. For me, it substantiated that God and science are in harmony, not conflict. And that's because God created science-like He created everything else.

I sensed that some of JM's motivation was that Kels had always prayed that the rest of her family would come to Christ, and if he could help us in that regard by being a teacher and a guide, then he was not only serving God, but honoring Kels. On Saturday, October 18, JM visited us, and he was particularly grieved that evening over losing Kelsey. His grief fueled my anger, and I went to bed frustrated and angry.

I heard a song by Brandon Heath entitled "Wait and See" that contained a line, "You're not finished with me yet.[18]" It resonated, although I failed to fully understand the implication. It is God that initiates, not us. My Type A, middle class, take charge personality told me that I was supposed to "do something."

Another song by Brandon Heath was extremely bittersweet. "Give Me Your Eyes" was a big hit for him[19]. Kelsey loved that song, and when she was in my car sitting next to me, she always changed the dial to K-love or Air One. When "Give Me Your Eyes" came on, she sang with it. The first Christian CD I purchased was Brandon Heath's, and when that song played, I could almost feel Kelsey next to me. I would turn and look at the passenger seat and was almost surprised when Kelsey was not there.

Another song I heard was "Whatever You're Doing" by Sanctus Real[20]. The first line was "It's time for healing, time to move on." In October, I was not ready for healing or moving on. Later, other parts of this song had more relevance.

In late October, I decided I would be re-baptized. I had been baptized when I was fourteen, and I had come to believe that Jesus was Christ, but I felt I needed to be re-baptized as a statement that I was starting a new journey. Pastor McMeans had read *From Ayn to Awe*, and he suggested that in light of my past deistic doubts that I should not call it a re-baptism, just a baptism. I chuckled, but I thought he had a valid point.

To me baptism was not a declaration that I knew all the answers; rather, that I would *seek* the answers, I would let God show me the answers. It was a testament of faith, and therefore, trust that God would reveal His truth in His time. I was still far from a deep and abiding trust, but it was a beginning.

On the last day of October, I purchased a Zondervan NASB Study Bible. I spent Halloween Night reading from Proverbs, Kelsey's favorite book. For the first time in my life, I was reading the Bible not to invalidate it, but to learn from it. Tell me that God isn't patient. He meets us where we are, not where we should be.

"We can look at this tragedy," JM told me, "as something that stopped our walk with God, or we can see that we are not alone, and that God created each of us for a special and unique purpose. Kelsey's death can stop us, or it can allow us to see the many aspects of our loving Father, who wraps us up in His arms when we have no other place to go."

Such was our choice in the month of October 2008.

Chapter Nine
November-December
Visits

*"Therefore the Lord himself will give you a
sign. Behold, the virgin shall conceive and bear
a son, and shall call his name Immanuel."*
Isaiah 7: 14

November and December proved to be the most volatile months.
Both good and bad. And while the bad was the most obvious, the
good was the most profound.

During this time Becky drew her strength from Christian music
on the radio. "Every time I was down, I'd hear some song, some
song that seemed to speak just to me. It would lift me up for at least
a little while. Over and over this occurred. I don't know how many
times that happened, but it helped me to keep going."

For me during the last two months of 2008, anger began
bubbling to the surface with ever more frequency and intensity, and
yet there were a few moments of profound joy. Ever so slowly the
mix of bad days and tolerable days gravitated towards the latter.
The intensity of the grief abated some, which prompted a measure
of guilt. Was I already forgetting Kels? And yet I could be brought
to tears in a flash.

It amazed me how quickly my emotions could change. A good
day would be followed by a bad one; a tolerable morning could

give way to a sad afternoon. Some times it changed in a matter of minutes. Anger and calm operated in juxtaposition, as did apathy and urgency. I was a churning cauldron of emotions. In my deist days, I had read some of the works of existentialist writer, Fyodor Dostoyevsky, who once wrote that we should be "worthy of our sufferings.[21]" At that time I thought that was very profound. Now it simply seemed profane. Nothing in this grief felt noble.

I still struggled not to conclude that our lives had not been ruined, and I feared we would never reach that "new normal" about which Darla Dunn had spoken. Retiring in May looked probable, not just possible. I just did not have the energy or focus at a time I needed both in significant quantities to conclude one construction bond issue and design another one that was two and half times larger. Sleep was still a difficult endeavor, and I had come to rely on two Tylenol PMs to put me under. By now I was chronically tired. I had heard of people in similar situations that slept to avoid the pain. I envied their ability.

At one point, I began indulging in an absurd weighing of grief. Someone, I told myself, that lost a child at three did not suffer as much as those of us who had eighteen years to become more attached. On the other hand, someone who lost a child to a long illness suffered more than us because the anticipation of death was drawn out. Parents who lost more than one child suffered more than us. On and on it went in twisted scenarios until I finally shook my head and said enough! What's the point!? Tragedy is tragedy, grief is grief. There are no balancing scales to weigh it.

On the other side of that line of thinking, I tried to have the perspective that we should be glad that at least we had Kelsey for eighteen years, but honestly any acceptance of that line of thought was usually short-lived. Most of the time, I was flooded with the sense of loss and a growing anger that fermented inside me.

For instance, how Kelsey died became kindling for my burgeoning anger. Trina Ehlers had told us that it was a blessing that Kelsey had been doing everything she should have been, and for a while that was how I looked at it. However, as the weeks wore on, those facts began to fill me with a rage: Kelsey had been doing what she should have been, but she had been killed anyway. Neither the president of the company nor the driver had ever been man enough to personally apologize. They sent a message through their attorney, which seemed cowardly and pathetically inadequate. A part of me wanted revenge. Forget that naïve, idealistic nonsense about forgiving and turning the other cheek. I wanted them to go to jail and die destitute.

In the study of psychotherapy at Texas Tech, I had learned that anger was a secondary emotion; that is, a derivative of something more powerful: fear. If that is the case, then November and December were the months of fear - fear of the unknown; fear that the future would always be as bad as the present; fear that we would not heal. Fear manifesting in anger. At these moments, my faith was more of a hope instead of a trust. I was angry, and frankly, it felt good. It was a way of standing up for us and for Kels.

A flourish of anger could erupt in an instant. I would be at my desk and think about Kelsey and would slam my fist on the desk. I even found myself angry at Kelsey. Why didn't you swerve earlier!? Just a half-second!

I tried not to resent it when I saw happy families with their kids, but a little bitterness inevitably crept in, particularly when I saw twins. Furthermore, I would see some kid on the news do some bad thing or read a criminal background check on a perspective employee, and I would think: these people hurt others, and yet they live on. Kelsey loved people and is dead. Where's the justice in that?

Two particular events demonstrated the amount of anger filling me. On November 11, JM turned twenty, and we went to his home for a birthday party. It hurt us to see John Michael. Pain seemed to seep from every part of him. An overpowering sense of loss ate at me. They had been cheated out of a life time together. I writhed with anger. "I desperately wanted to get out of there," Bec said afterwards. "It hurt to see John Michael in so much pain."

"It just didn't feel right celebrating anything without her being there," John Michael wrote later. "Sometimes joy seemed to be a bad thing, and celebrating things in my life seemed to be wrong. However, I would learn over time that life is far greater and more magnificent than just the 50, 60, 70, or even just 18 years we get here. We have an eternity with Christ and with our Daddy God in Heaven, where we will absolutely be in Him, and He in us. In time, God showed me to stop feeling bad for having joy and celebrating. I began to understand that Kelsey was not missing her time here, and she was not mad at us for smiling every once and a while. This was one of the biggest things the Lord showed me over the year. Christ died to save us for eternity, not just for these years here. God's plan is huge, and it is so much bigger than I can see."

That said, on the night of November 11, it was hard for JM or any of us to have a long term perspective. That night the loss loomed. Hard, cold reality controlled.

As we left the Vestal home and walked to the car, I looked up and said out loud in an angry voice that was more of a growl, "There had better be a good reason for this." The depth of my anger startled me. It was the first time I had directed my rage straight at God.

The second event occurred the following week. I felt myself brimming with rage as I worked at my desk. I went to the high school auditorium to check on construction. As I approached, one of the construction workers nearly hit my car with some irrigation pipe. I slammed on my brakes, spewing gravel in all directions, got out, slammed my door, and yelled at the worker: "Watch where you're going or I will have you fired!" Then I stomped off. Several minutes later I found the site superintendent and asked him to find that worker. I apologized for my unjustified outburst, then I drove to the gravesite just two hundred yards away and had a melt down. I screamed at the top of my lungs at God: "Why!?" Over and over I yelled this. They probably heard me at school. I had heard Pastor McMeans quote Romans 8:28 how "all things work to the good." How, I wanted to know, did this work to the good? How!? I was too angry at this point to see how God was working on me.

The timing of these events demonstrates the volatility of my emotions. I was re-baptized on the 9th, JM's birthday was the 11th, my brother, Greg, and niece, Taylor, paid a wonderful surprise visit on the 14th, and my melt down at work was on the 17th. I oscillated up and down like a roller coaster. Since that time, I have mentioned these events to others and how angry I was at this point, and they said they did not notice it at the time. I'm very good at hiding. However, God was not fooled.

Most of the events of November and December centered around basketball, which for both of us offered a welcomed diversion. For an hour and half we almost felt normal again. Becky was the lead mom on the basketball booster club and was responsible for organizing team dinners, "goody" bags for away games, and decorating the locker room and bus. She dove into this role, going above and beyond. She wanted to show her support for Kayla and for the whole team that had done so much for us since the accident. It kept her very busy, a fact for which she was grateful. "I kind of kept myself numb," she told me. "I didn't want to feel anything, and keeping busy with basketball helped me do that." In December, we went to the Granbury tournament near Ft. Worth, and it was good for all of us to get away for a few days.

Yet, the basketball season was at times still a hollow and empty experience. The first scrimmage particularly hurt. Kelsey's absence was palpable. Kayla was the only senior that had been on the team since she was a sophomore, and leadership duties fell to her. I could tell at times that the extra burden of leading the team was stressful. She rose to the challenge and took charge of the team.

However, while her leadership was solid and her stoic visage on the court was inspiring, her play was often erratic: one game she was focused; the next, you could see that she was pressing, trying to play for herself and for Kelsey. I didn't help the situation. The season had taken on an added sense of urgency. I wanted them to win so badly. I wanted something to go well.

When I look back, actually more things were going well than it felt like at the time. As I mentioned, Greg and Taylor showed up at a basketball game. They flew in from Iowa, and Jeremy picked them up at the airport. It was a wonderful surprise. An old friend, Bryan Stringer, that I had not seen in a decade, also made a surprise visit. On senior night before the game, the football team presented us with a beautiful glass case placed on a tripod on the sideline. In the case was a Lubbock-Cooper football jersey with "Vines" and "15" on it, autographed by the entire team. At half-time the band marched and arranged itself into a giant "15." Lubbock-Cooper continued to pick us up.

On Thanksgiving Day, Becky, Kayla, Jeremy and I flew to Iowa to surprise my mom and reassure her that we were doing okay. It was during our stay in Iowa that Kayla opened up to her cousins and expressed a degree of guilt towards Kelsey. "Sometimes, I treated Kelsey more like a little sister than a twin. There is so much I would like to say to her and now cannot." It was an emotional trip for all of us, and even though I broke down during the family prayer before the meal, it was good to be with family.

In December I was negotiating with a real estate developer, Rex Robertson, to purchase land for an elementary building. He asked if it was okay with us if he named the entire housing development Kelsey Park. We were very touched and honored. A local basketball official, who had called some Lubbock-Cooper games, wrote us a letter praising us for being so strong, and then published a similar letter in the school newspaper of Lubbock Christian University.

On the 14th, we started receiving gifts at our front door every morning from a secret Santa: food, candy, hot chocolate, decorative pillows and blankets, plaques and wall ornaments, and an angel statue. It was the twelve days of Christmas, and we were amazed at the quality of the gifts. It was fun to try to guess who it was. None of us got it right. It turned out to be Marla Sterling, a Lubbock-Cooper teacher and mother of Paige, a close friend of the twins, and mother of Tyson, who had dated Kelsey for a few months in 2007.

On December 23 Greg and his entire family arrived. Christmas morning we planted an evergreen tree in the yard. The Vestals came over, and we gathered around the tree, while John Michael led us in prayer. It was not a joyous Christmas. However, it was a thankful one. We were thankful for each other, thankful for God's loving hand. "There were so many times," JM said, "when Thom's smile and Becky's hugs would be enough to keep me pushing forward to the next day." Christmas was one of those days.

The following day we visited Carlsbad Caverns in New Mexico. It felt good to get away for a day with Greg and his family.

So despite the pervasive sadness that hung over all of us every day like a stationary front and the writhing anger that churned inside me, and to some degree, all of us, there were good moments in the last two months of 2008. However, it was God that provided the best.

I started reading one chapter of the Bible a day, usually before I went to the office, starting with Proverbs, Kelsey's favorite book. Over the next few months, I turned to Luke, Acts, and then Romans. While biblical inerrancy was still an issue for me, I discovered that it was not a deal-killer like it used to be (mainly because I had wanted it to be). In the past, any doubt or discrepancy raised a road block. Now I read on, and gleamed what I could, implicitly trusting that God would teach and reveal in His way in His time.

What was also different now was that I had two rocks upon which to stand (and to which I constantly came back). First, simple, but sheer logic dictated that there was a supernatural power that created the universe out of nothing. In December 2008, I read an article in *Discover Magazine* entitled, "A Universe Built For Us," by Tim Folger[22]. "Our universe seems inexplicably well designed for life," the article started. It's not inexplicable, I wanted to scream. There is a clear explanation. Physicist Andrei Linde was quoted in the article as saying, "We have a lot of really, really strange coincidences, and all of these coincidences are such that they make life possible." It's not a coincidence! I wanted to yell again. It's simple logic. At some point, some type of matter had to be created out of nothing. Science simply does not have an explanation for the initial genesis, for the utter complexity of the universe and the life in it, and the reason it does not is because it was not science that was the force of creation. It was beyond our natural laws. It was *super*natural. It was God.

I showed John Michael the article, and we discussed its theological implications. "I think I want to work with skeptics someday," I told him. I remember him breaking into a wide smile.

Second, I believed (as Josh McDowell pointed out) that Jesus was the Christ because his disciples would not have died for a lie. The disciples knew the truth, were transformed by it, and were subsequently willing to go to their deaths rather than deny it.

Those two convictions (both really logical deductions) became my foundation. If I had lost a child during my deistic days, without believing in both of those pillars, I probably would have collapsed and spiraled into atheism. But now these two core beliefs propelled me forward, and despite that tragedy and the tears, there was no turning back.

We attended Indiana Avenue nearly every Sunday, and for the first time in my life, I actually looked forward to going to church. It was a learning opportunity. I still failed to understand that as important as learning is, it is not the primary purpose of a service. It is called a worship service for a reason.

I think a fair statement is that my beliefs (then and even now) were based on reasoning, not blind faith. I did not easily believe in *anything*. I have a skeptical nature, which is why trust is so hard for me. That said, I moved towards God. However, I realized that I could not seek God just because Kelsey would have wanted it that way, or it was a way to see Kelsey again; rather, I had to seek God for my own benefit, as an end in itself. I had to seek God because He was God. At that point, I did not love God as much as I should, or as much as I would later; rather, I respected His position and feared His power. I had much to learn and to grow into.

It was a time of growth for John Michael, as well. "Despite the sorrow of November and December," he wrote, "I was growing, as was everyone who had been involved with this whole circumstance. There were many people that only knew of Kelsey and partially knew of me, and yet I was able to talk with them about the Lord and about where the Lord had taken me. God had used this to open numerous doors for all of us to share His love, His relentless and everlasting love for us, with random, yet perfectly placed people."

Much of my growth centered on reading. Besides reading chapters from the Bible each day, I re-read *The Shack* and *90 Minutes in Heaven*, and parts of Josh McDowell's *More Than a Carpenter*, Rick Warren's *The Purpose-Driven Life*[23], and C.S. Lewis's *Mere Christianity*. John Michael gave me a copy of Watchman Nee's *The Normal Christian Life* for Christmas- best Christmas gift I've ever received[24]. Watchman particularly helped me to understand the crucifixion and the role of blood. For those that say there are no more revelations and there are no more prophets after John finished the Book of Revelation, I give you Watchman Nee. So I read and re-read, and it was edifying and enriching, but that was not the best part.

In early December, Becky and I attended a meeting at Kyle Edwards's home with evangelist Sam Soleyn, a man of deep faith, profound insight, a piercing intellect and affable nature. I think Sam is another one of those modern-day prophets. Sam talked with us for nearly two hours. At first, his focus was more on Becky, and he immediately saw that despite her pain, her faith was very strong. "I'm not worried about you," he said. "You will do all right in time."

It was me about which he was more worried. After about five

minutes, he had me pegged: I was logical and suspicious of the mystic. "I have a law degree," he said, "and was trained to think logically, but faith is much more than an intellectual exercise." He told me of an experience where he was driving down the Interstate 20 west of Ft. Worth. "I was not thinking about anything in particular, when suddenly I had a mystic experience in which the Holy Spirit lifted me up and out of the car, as the car continued to speed down I-20. I hovered over it for sometime."

I could tell he was dead-on serious. I related to him an experience I had in the early 90's (the height of my deistic days), in which I sensed the death of a former student before it happened. I kept thinking of this student throughout the day- couldn't get him off my mind, even while sitting through a lecture, a lecture that I was interested in by a professor I admired, Dr. Nevius. After class I was walking through the parking lot of the Texas Tech book store and thought I saw this ex-student in a parked car. I went up to the car and realized it was not that student. The following day I learned the student had been killed on the campus of Texas A&M in the hours after I had these premonitions. This telepathic experience really shook me at the time, and I still do not know completely what to make of it. Obviously, I do not think it was a coincidence, and the experience confirmed to me that the laws of science do not explain everything.

Sam's main advice to me was to concentrate on the words "Holy Spirit" as I read the Bible, and in that way connect to the "non-linear" part of Christianity. Sam finished by saying "big changes" where coming our way. I felt the urge to say: hasn't that happened already? He went on to add that they were positive changes, and if we knew how big, we would run from them.

Another positive event occurred on November 9 when I was re-baptized. It was particularly rewarding to publicly humble myself before God. I stood on the steps overlooking the baptismal basin and looked out at the congregation. Sitting just below me was my family and the Vestals. Becky had a smile on her face. "Your baptism," she told me, "brought me a sense of peace. I knew how far you had come." John Michael was crying. Out of joy. I remember I had a big smile on my face, and I wished Kels could be there to see it. Who knows? Maybe she was. "Kels," Kayla told me afterwards, "prayed for a long time for this moment."

At the end of the service, Becky, Kayla, Todd and I joined the church. I did not know Todd was joining until that moment. Kayla never thought to tell us. She just did it. That was so like her, which is to say, it was so like me.

Both of those experiences deepened my understanding and faith, but even baptism was not the best part.

So what could be better than that? Sometime after meeting with Sam, I was driving down Indiana Avenue not far from the church when I started smiling. A wide, beaming, ear-to-ear smile. What am I smiling about!? I asked myself in wonder and indignation. Kelsey is dead and I'm smiling. Then I felt a wonderful swelling sensation inside me that was complete and utter joy, and I realized I was in the presence of the Holy Spirit. It was like the ultimate adrenaline rush. Of all the days and events since September 2, this was one of the best moments. C.S. Lewis entitled his autobiography *Surprised by Joy,* and that described me completely[25]. I drove the rest of the way home overwhelmed by the depth of joy running through me. I told myself at the time: this must be what Kels is feeling every moment.

"Thom had a joy about him that was unexplainable," John Michael later wrote. "He would talk about the Lord with me, and this grin would come on his face, and it was like he couldn't even help it. Isn't that how it's supposed to be? When we talk about the one true God, shouldn't we be so overwhelmed with joy that we just really can't help but grin?"

"So many of these nights," JM went on to say, "were filled with tears of joy. I saw God's hand in all of this. I saw Romans 8:28, and how He is for our good through it all. There is a song that reminds me of the many nights that I spent on the floor crying out to the Lord and receiving Him. It's called *How He Loves Us,* and it was written by John Mark McMillan and sung beautifully by Kim Walker[26]. There is a line that says 'Heaven meets earth like a sloppy wet kiss.' This image of Heaven invading my room and God coming down like the amazing and huge daddy God He is and kissing me. What a wonderfully crafted image of the love of our great and mighty God."

So John Michael and all of us to varying degrees discovered there was joy amidst the heartache. Furthermore, I discovered I trusted God more than I thought. I trusted Him to take care of

Kelsey. I trusted Him that He had provided a portal to salvation through Jesus Christ. I trusted Him enough that I was trying to obey His laws (though the purpose of the Law is to show we cannot do it by ourselves). And I trusted that in His time, He would provide answers to my many questions.

But then something would happen, some blimp on the radar screen, and I realized I still did not trust Him enough to *rely* on Him. I had been raised to be self-reliant. Relying on anybody or anything was an abdication of personal responsibility.

From that you can see why I had difficulty accepting the notion of grace. What do you mean it's a gift? I don't have to do anything? I don't have to earn salvation? How is that fair? How is that right? I want to *do* something.

Trust and self-reliance are inevitably antithetical tenets. At this point, I did trust God enough to seek Him, though I did not yet understand that it is He that seeks me. But seeking is not the same as relying. I was like that stray dog that tagged along behind a potential master: I'll follow where you go, but I'm not going to get too close, and if you do something I don't understand, I'm history.

For the same reason prayer was still problematic for me. I could pray for forgiveness- for which I surely needed, but as Watchman Nee pointed out: it's already been provided through Christ's finished work on the cross. He emphasized praise over prayer. I still felt that praying for some ability, end reward, or even help in one's faith was like cheating- although like the hypocrite I was, I still prayed for those things. And getting close to God? That was entirely my task.

I still didn't get it.

Furthermore, I did not yet trust Him to ensure there would be no more tragedy. As the months wore on from Kelsey's killing, it was that that bore on my heart and mind: please God, I can't do this again. But from this plea, I got no sense of response.

This type of dread also ate at Becky. Once while at school, an ambulance roared down Indiana Avenue heading south. Bec called me. "I'm really spooked." I called Kayla to make sure she was okay, then called Becky back. When Bec came home, she was still pale and clearly flustered.

The following week I met with Darla Dunn. She had established a scholarship in honor of her son, Stephen Starch, a 1990 Lubbock-Cooper graduate and a first rate Christian man. We discussed the organization of her scholarship fund, but the salient memory I have of that meeting is how easily the grief came back to her- after 11 years. I remember thinking: is this how I will be in 2019?

Nights of hard grief still swarmed us. The night of December 18 attacked Bec, and I comforted her. Three nights later I was the one under assault, and she comforted me. Neither of us said anything in particular. We just held each other and listened to the rage that spilled from the other.

On the 23rd, Greg and his family arrived. The following night, Christmas Eve, Kelsey came to Becky. In my deistic days, if Becky had told me this story, I would have said "bull" and other words that go with bull. As she was saying her nightly prayers, Kelsey appeared before her. There was a glow about her, and she was more beautiful than ever. Kelsey said, "Mom, I'm okay. I'm really okay," and disappeared. Becky knew she was awake. "It was *not* a dream," she said emphatically. "It was a gift, a wonderful gift." She told me about it a few days later.

My initial reaction? Jealousy. Why didn't Kelsey come to me, too? I wanted to see her. I wanted to know she was okay.

Then came New Year's Eve. I had expected Christmas to be tough, and I was mentally prepared for it. I was not prepared for the broadside of the last hours of 2008. For the previous three days, we had attended a basketball tournament, so that by the evening of the 31st, I had seen enough high school girls' basketball and did not wish to go to still another game. So Becky went to games with Shanna Edwards, and I stayed home alone.

Between reading from the Book of Acts, I flipped through the channels while watching the clock click towards midnight. As the hourglass of 2008 spilled towards empty, I realized that before long Kelsey would no longer have been alive during the current year. I still don't know why that mattered so much, but it did. It hit me hard, and I sat alone in my living room wailing as the last seconds of 2008 ticked away.

John Michael wrote of this time. "These were the months when I stopped asking why so often and replaced it with when. When would God's hand be visible in everything that I've gone through? This question and the hope of the answer would keep my journey going and provided me the strength to make it through each day. There was no explanation for how we made it through each day, but yet we did. I cannot explain to someone how God did it, but what I can say is that God's love never fails, and it's because of this fact that we make it through those dark valley's and make it to the mountain tops once again."

2008: the worst year of our lives. And yet, a little voice whispered between my cries that something else was beginning, that we were all part of something else bigger than any us. And through it all ran the conviction that somehow Kelsey's death would glorify God and His purpose. But how?

Kayla kissing Kelsey.

JM and Kelsey on her 18th birthday.

One of my favorites: the "goofy" side of Kelsey.

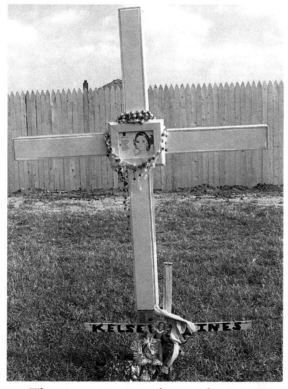

The two crosses at the accident site.

Kesley's grave

Homecoming 2008

Kayla wearing Kelsey's jersey.

April Ehlers, Kayla, Kimberly Harger, and Brandi DeWaters wearing "Kelsey t-shirts" in the basketball locker room.

The Memorial Garden

Kelsey giving the "I love you" sign.

Chapter Ten
Early 2009
A Spring Flurry

"Praise be to God and the Father our Lord Jesus Christ! In his great mercy he has given us new birth into a living hope through the resurrection of Jesus Christ from the dead."
1 Peter 1:3

The year 2009 came in, as they say, like a lion: a day of hard grief. New Year's Eve spilled into New Year's Day with a few hours of sleep in between. By now I was concluding that there were not going to be good days, just bad ones and tolerable ones. I thought of what Ronnie Quest had told me: "It's not going to get better." Maybe he's right I told myself. I was still longing for that "new normal" of which Darla Dunn spoke, or was it already here, and I just did not want to accept that this was the way it was going to be for the rest of our lives? Bec had already said she feared that it was never going to get any better. Maybe she was right.

Everyday brought some challenge, some bigger than others; but at least once every waking hour I thought of Kelsey, at least once every day I had a "Kelsey moment," at least once a week I had a good cry, and once a month I still imploded. Grief, though not as frequent or severe, was becoming a way of life.

What was amazing was the power of denial. I would see Kelsey's photograph, of which there were dozens in our home and

107

in my office, and I would still have to remind myself that it really happened. I told Ronnie Quest that I believed a good hypnotist could take me into a secluded room and convince me that it never happened, that it was all a bad dream. I wanted to believe it was a bad dream. Such is the power of the subconscious; such is the hold of grief.

Becky was experiencing the same thing. "Somehow I was hoping it was like an episode in the television show 'Dallas,'" she told me. "It was all going to turn out to be a bad dream, and Bobby was taking a shower and everything was okay. I knew better, but there was a part of me that vainly hoped for this." I felt the same way. I often fantasized about going back in time and stopping the accident, making everything all right.

Our denial was augmented by another continuing psychological dynamic. I became aware over time that I used grief to stay close to Kelsey. At times when I felt sad or angry, I sensed the presence of Kelsey, as if she was right there trying to comfort me. This was cemented by the fact that if I did not feel sad, if I allowed myself to laugh or enjoy a moment, I felt guilty. Somehow I was letting Kelsey down. I was abandoning her.

Grief is not always a rational process. It is certainly not linear. It is sporadic, with an ebb and flow of its own. It is up, down, and around. For a stretch of time, it will seem to be slowly, but steadily declining in its intensity, and then from out of nowhere it hits you. It spikes. It attacks. So grief is defiant and resilient, and yet at times a strange kind of friend, like an enemy that you need that spurs you on to something you must do. That is why grief is so necessary.

In graduate school at Texas Tech, I had read a paper on a meta-analysis of the leading therapy methods. I do not remember the name of the article or the author. The researcher studied all the major therapies from Freud to Skinner and many in between and concluded that no one therapy proved to be completely effective in all circumstances. In fact, the most powerful curative agent of all was the simple passage of time.

Time, I rolled over in my mind. I have to put in my time. Is that all there is to it? Or is this a life sentence? And then a little voice: ...do you want it to be?

For Becky, time meant another day of going through the motions. "I numbed myself and just got through each day. I did whatever was required and then went home, home to a house where Kelsey was supposed to be, but wasn't. And yet in a way, she was. I didn't care to go out to the gravesite. That was not her. She was not there. I felt her in our home. That's where Kelsey was."

The only thing that flowered for Bec during this winter of languor and anguish was her faith, and the fulcrum for that faith often continued to be Christian music. Christian music lifted her and brought her in touch with her feelings, with her pain.

Like Kels and JM, Bec's faith was relational. Mine was intellectual, theirs was relational. A relationship with Christ. Bec was slowly, but surely learning to rely on Christ. While I continued to struggle, she steadily strengthened. Accordingly, I started turning to her. Leaning on her. On her strength. On her faith.

"There are many times we want to deal with grief and sorrow on our own, but this is not what God intends," John Michael wrote me later. "You see, everything we go through in our lives God allows in order for us to see Him more clearly. Even though I could not see it deep down at the time, I knew that my God had allowed all this to happen in order for Him to be glorified. For instance, I was able to share my story with many people. It was not that God took Kels in order to hurt us, but in order to bring Romans 8:28 to fullness in our lives. I did not realize this immediately, and it took many nights of praying and fighting with the Lord. But steadily, He began to break through my grief."

In January 2009, I started attending "D-team" (discipleship) meetings at IABC, led by Johnny Vestal, John Michael's father. Most of the group was college kids in various stages of faith. They were very impressive and reinforced in me that, in knowledge of the Bible, I was a complete neophyte. Becky and I also attended a Wednesday night class on the Book of Mark, where I saw for the first time "The Passion of the Christ.[27]" Very powerful and excruciating. Its graphic parts reminded me of "Saving Private Ryan.[28]"

As John Michael and I grieved together and now studied the Bible together, the bond between us grew and deepened. "We were beginning to form a brother-like relationship," JM wrote. "It was something like that of many of the disciples in the Bible. He called me his spiritual leader, yet ironically, I kept telling my family that he was mine."

By now, I visited the gravesite only once or twice a week. It did not have the hold on me that it once had. She's not really there, I would tell myself. That's just her earthly body. I would imagine her corpse lying in the casket six feet below slowly decaying, and then I imagined the dump truck coming at them and her frozen face of horror. Then I would try to imagine her in heaven relying on Don Piper's book for some type of image, but it was so abstract in comparison to the hard reality of the grave at my feet.

One day while I visited the gravesite during the spring semester, Amanda Kitten, a senior and friend of the twins, was there. It comforted me to know that she would take the time to visit. She asked if I came to the gravesite everyday, and I said, "Not any more."

Kayla started designing the memorial garden. Seniors at Lubbock-Cooper are required to do a senior project. The first semester is a research paper, and the second is a hands-on project supplementing the research. Before the accident, Kayla was going to do tap dancing (she could not think of anything else). After the accident, there was only one thing for her to do: build a memorial to her twin.

Her research paper had been on the unique challenge of losing a twin. The project was a memorial garden on school grounds, which Pat approved. Most schools would not have allowed such a project for it was overtly Christian. Each project must have a mentor, and Kayla's was Joe Gillespie, who headed Lubbock-Cooper's Grounds Department. In January Kayla, Todd and Joe started laying out the initial idea for the garden.

January was a tough month for Kayla. On the 21st, she finally wrote about Kelsey in her blog on My Space.

> "...This year I lost my twin sister in a terrible car accident. I never thought that something this tragic would happen to my family or me. Was it because I was naïve? Maybe. Or maybe it was because I just went through the motions of life and only thought of myself. ...I wake up each morning realizing that my beautiful twin sister is not here anymore. I feel so empty and lost without her at my side. A twin is a privilege, a partner for life. ...Life is hard. There

is no doubt about that. But it is how we cope with the challenge that makes us the person we are meant to be. I know that Kelsey would want me to work hard and live my life to the fullest. I must do that for her and also for myself. Kelsey touched the lives of so many people. She lived her life as everyone should. She showed people that they should live their lives through God, and that He is the only way. Sometimes people lose sight of that. Kelsey always had a way of reminding them. Her favorite verses were Matthew 6:34 and Proverbs 3:5. Kelsey was such a beautiful person with a strong and passionate heart. She captured so many with her smile. She was a talented photographer with a bright future. She loved God more than anything. She had a childlike personality. That is what I loved about her the most. She will be my hero forever. Through this year I have matured and so has my faith in our Lord and savior Jesus Christ. God has been my rock. Kelsey showed me to have a strong faith and give God the glory. God has something big in store for my life, and one day may I join Him and live in heaven for all eternity. I loved Kelsey so much and miss her everyday. I know that she is with me all the time, and she is looking over me. We had eighteen years together, and I cherish every single day. Kelsey saved my life, and we will be together again some day. Maybe not now; maybe sixty years from now, but I know she will be waiting for me at the gates of heaven. And then I will be home."

It was moving, touching, and tough to read, but rewarding to see how Kayla's faith had flowered. God was using her just as He was using Becky and me.

One of the ways Kayla dealt with the loss of her twin was taking an interest in photography, including taking photographs for the school newspaper, one of Kelsey's roles. We noticed that she made a significant effort to get it right, just as Kelsey did. As

111

usual, Kayla never mentioned any of this. She just quietly went about her task.

I also found that I was aware of photographs more than usual. I would see a good shot and say to myself: that sure is a nice picture. Kelsey could have done that. Then a little voice: but she never will get to.

Kayla's basketball play continued to be erratic and at times lackluster. She had always been the one named to the hustle award, mainly because of her defensive play. But now she was going through the motions. I sensed she longed for the season to be over. At the end of the month, Kayla and I discussed the situation. I told her she had one month left. How did she want to go out? She re-dedicated herself and started spending extra time in the gym after scheduled practices.

There were special moments of grief in January. Darrell Ericson, a new assistant principal at Lubbock-Cooper's Middle School, lost his father in a car accident. Attending that funeral brought back painful memories of Kelsey's funeral, and I spent that night ensconced in hard grief.

On the 24th, Becky thought she was having a heart attack. It turned out to be "only" grief. Like me the day before Kelsey's funeral, grief became so acute that it simulated the symptoms of a coronary. Four and a half months after Kelsey's death, the grief was at times still that strong and stinging.

February was an emotional month. On the 9th, we received in the mail from Governor Perry the Texas flag that flew over the Texas capitol on the day of Kelsey's funeral. We did not know it was coming. Governor Perry also sent along a nice memorial plaque. Becky and I were very touched by this.

Meanwhile, we started raising money for the memorial. Kayla and I taped a spot on KRFE radio that would be played during Lubbock-Cooper athletic events. Later, we went on their morning show to thank everyone for their help. The memorial ended up costing over $20,000, and the contributions covered every cent and then some. It was incredible. The extra money helped fund the scholarship program.

As part of funding-raising for the memorial, Alexandra Nanny helped Kayla sell red t-shirts. On the front it read "Kelsey Vines,

Matthew 6:34," and on the back was a large "15." They sold over 600 t-shirts and made over $5,000 for the memorial.

The last home game of district play was Senior Night where the senior players and their parents are introduced and recognized. Dozens of people in the stands wore their red Kelsey Vines t-shirts. Once more the news was there. Because our last name began with a "V," we went last in the introduction of the seniors. That was the only thing we knew that was going to happen that night. Kayla, Becky and I emerged from the tunnel, and then Darrell Bednarz announced that at the behest of the basketball team, Kelsey's jersey was retired- except for that night: Kayla would wear the jersey of her twin. Obviously, it was a very emotional evening, and Kayla's and the team's play was uneven, as well, like their emotions. They eeked out a narrow, stressful victory.

Months later, Becky told me that she had regretted that Senior Night was so much about Kelsey. "As grateful as I was for everything, I wanted Senior Night to be about all the senior girls, including Kayla and Kelsey. I wanted it to be a thank you to the whole team and all the fans. I appreciated all the honors going to Kelsey, but there was a part of me that did not want to be reminded about it. Basketball was supposed to be a diversion from the pain, and at times it was another reminder. Of course, at the time I didn't say anything because I didn't want people to get the wrong idea and think I was ungrateful. I most certainly was not. But at times, everything was so public that I just couldn't grieve by myself."

The basketball team finished as Co-District Champions and moved into the play-offs. Now each game could be their last. Kayla re-invigorated her game and was now playing the best basketball of her career. I was proud of her for raising the level of her play and going out with style and class.

At the Regional Tournament, Lubbock-Cooper defeated a very good Bridgeport team in overtime and faced district rival and co-champion, Lubbock Estacado in the Regional Finals for the right to go to the State Tournament in Austin. No Lubbock-Cooper girls' basketball team had ever made it to State. We did not have one of our best games and lost by two points. It was heartbreaking.

After the game, the team knelt before the Lubbock-Cooper crowd for one last photograph, and they gave the "I love you" sign that Kelsey always made. On my screen saver in my office I have three photographs: one of Kayla and Kelsey when they were very young sitting together in a laundry basketball and Kayla is kissing Kelsey; a second is one with Kelsey in goggles making a goofy face (pure Kelsey); and the third is Kelsey giving the "I love you" sign (it is similar to the Texas Longhorns sign), and there is a glow of light surrounding her. All these photographs are also in this book. When the team gave the "I love you" sign, I lost my veneer of composure and cried for a few seconds.

We had little down time, which was both a blessing and a burden. The building of the memorial garden consumed March, as did the organizing of the Kelsey Vines Memorial Scholarship. Mentor Joe Gillespie led the way on the memorial, getting many contractors to donate money, material, or labor. The garden would not have been built without Joe's help. The contributors included Laredo Concrete, Acme Brick, Jordanville Landscaping, Sandia Construction, TG Trees, Teague Landscaping, All Seasons Property Care, Innovative Landscapes, KRFE Radio, Balfour Graduation Services, Jamie McCann, Roy Heinrich, Frankie Justice, and Dr. Jim Wetherbe, who donated his "Faith Logic" book to sell. Of particular note is Sadler Monument, who donated a beautiful granite bench with a mahogany granite basketball. It is the center piece of the memorial.

Besides my family, Joe, and JM, workers included Todd and Les Howell, the Kyle Edwards family, the Vestals, the Alan Vinsons, the Ehlers, Kimi Harger, Bill Jackson, the Lubbock-Cooper grounds crew, and a crew from Joe's All Seasons Property Care. As you can see, it was a group effort. Nearly everyday after school, on weekends, and all spring break there was work of some type going on- hundreds of man-hours in all. It became a project in which all of us could channel our grief.

Like the memorial, the scholarship was a lot of work, but it was also a wonderful way to express our gratitude to the community. It felt good to do something positive, and it took some of the sting out of Kelsey's death. Over $14,000 was contributed to the scholarship fund by people inside Lubbock-Cooper and outside, as well. We funded two $2,000 scholarships each year. As part of the scholarship award, I had House Foundry make a bronze medallion based on the Kelsey flag the football team had created. I had twenty made, so we made a ten year commitment to the scholarship.

Ten LCHS seniors applied, and as I looked through the applications the first time, I turned to Donna Hanfeld, the high school counselor, and said, "We have a tough decision to make." There was not a single throw-away in the entire batch, and there were seven that finished near the top of the rating system. It was a very close count.

During March, the new Performing Arts Center was finally completed. As the Deputy Superintendent in charge of bond construction, I was very proud how it turned out. One of the first events was the district one-act play competition, and Lubbock-Cooper presented "The Women of Lockerbie," a play about the agony of losing a child in a plane crash[29]. It was a wonderful performance, but very tough to watch, in part because the acting was so well done. It also served to demonstrate how nearly everything reminded me of losing Kelsey. Losing Kelsey was the prism through which I now viewed life.

When Kelsey was alive, John Michael and I had a good relationship, but not a close one. I think each looked on the other with a bit of a jaundiced eye: I at the boy dating my daughter, he at the stern daddy of his girlfriend. Spiritual issues further kept us at bay. He was clearly a devoted Christian, while I was a fledging young colt, still unsure and unstable in my Christian walk. We had a few religious discussions, but nothing deep or long.

Of course, that all changed on September 2. We were thrown together- first in shock, then in hard grief. Through the autumn of 2008, the relationship slowly turned towards spiritual issues and questions. As I mentioned before, I sensed that JM, as a way of honoring both Kels and God, wanted to be our spiritual guide; he dreamed of leading all of us into heaven with Kelsey standing there, smiling and giggling as she always did.

This leadership started with the video on laminin, proceeded to my baptism, discussions about the *Discover* magazine article on creation, and included his Christmas gift of Watchman Nee's book. At that time, he wrote me a wonderful letter.

> "I can't tell you how much of a blessing it is to get to witness the transformation of a life happening right before my eyes to my sweetheart's dad. Continue to allow the Lord to work in your life. It's such an

awesome thing to watch. I love you. You are like a
dad to me."

At the time I was very touched by the letter, and as the months
rolled on I found it meant even more to me.

While I very much believed in God's loving hand and that Jesus
of Nazareth was the Christ, I still battled with the issue of Biblical
inerrancy, particularly in regards to Genesis. This was much more
than some intellectual debate. For me, it drove deep to the issue
of trust. If my faith was to continue to flower, I had to trust the
Bible. All of it.

And I didn't.

Enter John Michael. Patient. Loving. Wise beyond his years.

He listened to my questions. He asked questions of his own.
He read my *From Ayn to Awe*. He suggested chapters and verses
for me to read. He quoted. He countered.

Maybe more important was what he did not do. He did not
rant or rave. He did not judge or jeer. But he did jostle. And he
did jab.

During March, I read a book review in *Newsweek* on "Jesus,
Interrupted" by Bart Ehrman[30]. I also googled his web site. He was
a former evangelical turned skeptic, primarily because he thought
the Bible had been accidentally, and even purposely, changed and
distorted- exactly what I used to believe in my deist days. One of
his arguments was that the claims by Jesus that he was the Son
of God were vague. I showed this to John Michael, and he shook
his head. "It's anything but vague." He pointed out that Jesus
called himself the "Son of Man" many times and "Son of God"
at least twice. I looked it up in the concordance, and sure enough,
Jesus referred to himself as the "Son of God" in Mark 14: 61-2
and John 11:25, and as the "Son of Man" (an important phrase
in Jewish culture) over eighty times. I admit that I have not read
all of Ehrman's book, but I don't see the basis of his thesis. More
importantly, this investigation reinforced my faith that Christ was
exactly what He said He was.

Meanwhile, JM knew I had doubts about the legitimacy of
Genesis 1 and 2. I certainly believed creation was God initiated
(even the Darwinists don't really have an answer for the initial

spark of creation), but that left open the possibility of evolution as a method of God's work.

JM did not directly refute my assertion that God used evolution as His method; rather, he quoted 2 Peter 3:5 "...that with the Lord one day is like a thousand years, and a thousand years like one day." Actually, to me this confirmed the possibility of evolution, rather than negating it.

Then he rented a DVD by Ben Stein, "Expelled: No Intelligence Allowed," which was both entertaining and educating[31]. At one point, Stein asked a scientist how life started, and the scientist said that molecules clung to crystals. I wanted to scream at the screen: well, where'd the crystals come from!? And whatever answer he gave, I would have the same question, ad nauseum. Sheer logic dictated that at some point something had to be created out of nothing. Only a supernatural power could do that. Non-believers ask me why I believe in God, and I respond, "Logical deduction."

Still, that does not mean that evolution does not have legitimacy. Evolution could still be the *method* God chose. I could not let this go as just an intellectual disagreement. To me it was of fundamental importance because I saw it as the precept to the hinge of history. It was the "A" that led to the "B" in the Aristotlean syllogism. Let me explain.

Christ came to save a fallen world from its inherent sin. That's step B. That's the "hinge of history." The single most important event of the entire human story.

Why was the world "fallen?" That's step A. The traditional answer: because Adam and Eve disobeyed and ate the apple from the Tree of Knowledge. Original Sin.

But what if there was not a real Adam as described in Genesis? What if evolution of *some sort* took place, and Cro-Magnon Man gradually became some more modern model. What if there was not an actual Garden of Eden? What if Genesis 1 and 2 were only allegory, like other parts of the Bible? Did that mean it was not true? Did that mean there was no "Fall?" For if there was no "Fall," there was no need for a savior.

This was the heart of my dilemma, and it bothered me incessantly. I found myself oscillating from one side to the other.

One week I believed there was some type of evolutionary process. The next I believed in Genesis.

At this time, I also spoke with Reverend McMeans about this issue. I very much admired his pastoral leadership. He listened patiently, and then politely answered, "I believe in the inerrancy of all of God's word, including Genesis 1 and 2," although he did denote differences between the first chapter of Genesis and the second.

John Michael and I discussed this issue. He clearly believed there was an Adam, an Eve, and an Eden. And a Fall. I envied his clarity, but was determined that any resolution would be a matter of conviction, not convenience. As spring became summer, I was still very torn on this issue.

Another issue JM and I debated also came from Genesis: the Noah story. While not as important as the issue of a Fall, it still was a point of debate. Frankly, I did not consider Genesis 6-8 to be allegory. I considered it to be myth, particularly the part about Noah collecting male and female of every species from all over the world- including the Artic, the Antarctica, and Australia. I thought it was a silly story that undermined the credibility of the entire Bible- if one has to believe that it is 100% inerrant to trust it.

John Michael pointed out that it is possible that God brought animals from those regions close to where Noah was building his ark. I acknowledged that was a possibility, but added: then why didn't the Bible just say so. Again, not a major issue, and JM at least partially deflected my argument. More important than any one issue, we were developing a spiritual bond. He was becoming something more to me than just being the young man that my daughter loved.

And that more than anything is what JM taught me. God wants a relationship, not someone with the "right" answers. He and I still had debates. I saw God as the ultimate judge, while JM argued God was a God of love. Maybe both of us are right on that one. I found it hard to trust. JM pointed out that not trusting was a sin in itself.

He was a fervent leader of prayer and had a deep sense of connection to God. "God put on my heart..." he often said, while I did not feel a thing- or was too unaware to recognize God's signals. I envied him so much about this that sometimes I was almost mad about it. I wanted to hear God, too. Then I remembered reading how Watchman Nee waited seven years for a particular revelation. I realized patience mattered. God is on His time table, not ours. Sometimes He makes us wait. And then sometimes, as with the loss of Kelsey, He pushes us before we think we are ready. So, when I would say I have to seek God even more, JM taught me that it is God that leads and directs. We do not so much find God as God finds us.

JM and I did not always agree. We did not always like what the other said. But we grew together. And our relationship was no longer just about Kelsey. At first it was primarily that, but as time went on, it became about us; which is say, it became about Christ. Through Christ. In Christ.

One day in church in April, Shelley Vestal, JM's mom, showed me her Bible. She turned to Matthew 6:34, and next to it was written "September 2, 1990." The day Kelsey died in the year she was born. Furthermore, Shelley's Bible contained a note: "See Mark 5: 36," which reads "Don't be afraid. Just believe." On Monday, September 1, 2008, the last full day of Kelsey's life, Kelsey told JM of a new verse she was concentrating on besides Matthew 6:34. That verse was Mark 5:36. A string of coincidences? A lot of "really, really strange coincidences?"

Late March and early April was a mad, stressful dash to complete the memorial garden in time to dedicate it on the twin's birthday, April 7. Several dozen people worked long hours to get it done, led by mentor Joe Gillespie. Josh Jordan and his landscaping crew spent seven hours in 30 to 50 mile an hour winds laying down sand and paver bricks. Bill Jackson led a crew to build the arbor, completing it the morning of the 7th. Joe Gillespie and his crew, Les and Todd Howell, Kyle Edwards and family, and many others all put in long hours to make it possible. It became everyone's project, not just ours.

On the night of April 6, John Michael stayed in Kelsey's bed, the first time it had been slept in since the accident. The following day we dedicated the memorial garden despite strong winds. Once more the news covered the event. Two hundred attended, most of them wearing their red Kelsey t-shirts. As I stood next to the granite bench donated by Sadler Monument, I thanked all that had worked and donated materials or money. The community support was incredible. Alexandra Nanny gave some reminiscences of Kelsey, and John Michael led us in prayer.

For all of us, but particularly Kayla, the day was one of relief that the garden was finished, satisfaction that the dedication occurred on their birthday, and sadness for Kelsey's absence. It was Kayla's first birthday without her twin. Later, Kayla won the top award for the best senior project.

The following week Kayla and I went on KRFE once more to thank everyone for their help. The Lubbock-Cooper community seemed to come together around Kelsey. It was all very heartwarming.

The following night was heart wrenching. At D-team, JM read from his journal telling of his anguish and loneliness. I left the room angry. His pain always made me angry.

May was a flurry, a sprint to the end. On the 6th, my nephew, Jordan (Jason's son), arrived from Michigan to spend the next ten days with us. The 7th brought a broadside: one of our worst nights of hard grief. Becky lay on Kelsey's bed and writhed with agony: "She should be here; John Michael and she should be planning a wedding, planning a family..." I could not console her and had to call JM. When he arrived, I was sitting on the street curb, my head buried in my knees. He came in and helped us through our pain with a prayer that was more of a desperate plea.

On the 10th, Lubbock-Cooper had its athletic assembly. They ran a video of Kelsey's basketball play, and then presented us with one of her retired jerseys. Later, Darla Dunn awarded one of the Stephen Starch scholarships for Christian endeavor to Kayla. Of all the honors, that one was the one that meant the most to Kayla and to us.

Two days later, Sam Soleyn visited our home with Kyle Edwards and family. It was wonderful to hear him speak again. His insight into the Lord was amazing.

That evening was the high school awards assembly, and we announced the first winners of the Kelsey Vines Memorial Scholarship. For years, I had watched Darla Dunn award the scholarship in honor of her son, Stephen Starch. I could still vividly remember 1998 when she announced the first winners. Her voice was choked with emotion, and she struggled to get through the presentation. I remember thinking at the time: I cannot imagine what she is going through.

Now we were in the same position. As Becky, Kayla, John Michael and I walked to the podium, memories of Darla Dunn in 1998 flashed in my mind. Even though I had written out the entire speech and practiced it several times, I still struggled to maintain control as I worked my way to announcing the two winners. When I finally named the two recipients, Alexandra Nanny and Taylor Langston, I stepped back from the podium and a vision of Kelsey smiling at us filled my mind. We had done some good. We fashioned a modicum of triumph out of tragedy.

The final event of the evening was Mr. and Miss CHS. Kayla had been nominated by the faculty for Miss CHS, and in her essay she talked of her love for Christ. Kayla's faith had flowered in crisis. Amanda Kitten was named Miss CHS, and Kayla, Becky and I all believed Amanda had rightfully earned the honor.

The next evening, May 13, our D-team heard Sam Soleyn speak at a local Lubbock home. After the meeting with Sam in December, I had sent *From Ayn to Awe* to him and he had read it. During his talk, Sam said, "Some people waste a decade in doubt." When he said that he looked straight at me. I almost corrected him. I did not waste a decade. It was more like a quarter of a century. And yet, that time of deistic doubt and searching now served as a launching pad to a deeper and truer faith, and thus, I don't regret those years. In the vernacular of psychotherapy, I had reality-tested. When someone now talks of doubt, I know of what they speak. It's just a good thing that I did not die early.

As I was walking out of the home, a woman approached and asked if I remembered her. I recognized her, but could not remember her name. She, too, had lost a child: Justin, age seven, to cancer a year and a half ago. She told me of Justin's wonderful spirit and the difficulty of watching him waste away with cancer. She did not get explicit. She did not have to. There is a short hand that exists between parents who have lost a child. It is almost like you can finish their sentences. She said we seemed to have adjusted reasonably well, and she asked how we had learned to do it. I wanted to say: is that how it looks? I thought of last week when JM had to come to the rescue. I told her that it had been a very difficult time, and we tried to rely on God as much as possible, and some days we could do that, and, frankly, some we could not. When she left, she was still in tears, and I felt troubled that I had not done more to help her.

I ran into her again the next evening at a high school band concert. I had been thinking about our conversation all day and what I could have said better that may have provided a modicum of solace. I asked her for her mailing address so I could write her a letter, and she gave me her name, Tami Bolton. In the letter, I discussed our mutual anguish and how unfair it all was, and then I said we learned to do what Kelsey did: trust God.

Did I trust God? I asked myself as I wrote the letter. Yes, more than ever. I trusted God that He had taken Kelsey unto Himself. I trusted God that His grace would save me through His son. I trusted God would reveal His truth and answer my questions in His time. I trusted that God *was* the truth, *is* the truth. I *hoped* that there would be no more tragedy. I thought some more. Did I trust God on a daily basis to guide me and take care of all my problems? I thought about it, prayed on it, but I knew the answer. I still did not trust God enough to truly rely on Him in good times and bad and everything in between. The old self-reliant me was still very much in control.

Saturday, May 16, was prom night. Kayla went without Todd because he had already graduated, and she did not want him to be bored at a high school event. They had already attended two proms together. JM came over to see Kayla beforehand, and the memories of Kelsey and him a year ago were so vivid that I expected her to walk into the room any moment. I remembered how happy Kelsey was last year to be going to the prom with John Michael. It hurt more than ever that she was not there now, and I could see the pain behind JM's brave smile. Once more his pain made me angry.

Bec and I went to the prom on the campus of Texas Tech. For the last two years I had always danced with each of my daughters. This year I danced with Kayla once more, and Kelsey's absence hung over us.

On the 21st of May, I sat down with Reverend McMeans once more. I wanted to talk about forgiveness: my forgiveness of the company and driver that killed Kelsey. We were entering more detailed discussions with Armor's insurance company, and these issues weighed on my mind. I had re-read parts of *Man's Search for Meaning* by Viktor Frankl. Frankl had survived Auschwitz and knew that if he was to go on he had to find a way to forgive the NAZIs[32]. It was a powerful example.

I asked Pastor McMeans about forgiving Jimmy Hogan, owner of Armor Asphalt, and Pedro Alcorte, the driver, and he stated that as hard as it is, it is not a suggestion. It is a command. He offered several verses for me to read. However, he also noted that does not mean that there is not accountability. That is a different thing.

I discussed the issue of forgiveness and accountability also with John Michael. Like Pastor McMeans, he, too, said we all have to forgive. Then he added "Remember when you are thinking about a law suit, that this was all part of God's plan."

After he left, I reflected on the conversations with JM and Reverend McMeans. Was it God's plan? I asked myself. Invariably, I answered. I don't know why He allowed the accident, but clearly He did. Does that mean then that there is no accountability in human courts? I shook my head. The high school principal in me came out. There has to be a human measure of justice or our society implodes. Reverend McMeans was right, I told myself. Forgiveness and accountability were two different things. We would pursue accountability. And we would pursue forgiveness.

Was I ready to forgive them in my heart? I asked myself. I knew the answer before the thought fully formed in my mind. I was not even close. I was not even ready to discuss it with God.

On the 28th, Kathy and Rich arrived for Kayla's graduation. We showed them the road side crosses, the memorial and the grave marker, as well as the many things given us during the year: the flag from the Governor, the retired jersey, the honorary football jersey, and the flag the football team had made. Jason and his daughter, Lane, arrived the next day, and we showed them the same sites and memorabilia. They continued to be amazed by the support the community gave us.

Graduation was Saturday, May 30. We knew it would be an emotional day. As class vice-president, Kayla gave the prayer. By a new state law, a senior who died during the year and would have graduated in good standing could be awarded a diploma. After all the seniors had been given their diplomas, Kayla and I came forward to accept Kelsey's. The crowd rose to show their appreciation. It was a very bittersweet moment.

As tough as graduation was, it brought a measure of satisfaction and pride. We had made it through the year. As Paul writes in 2 Thessalonians, we had persevered, and we were thankful. Each of us had done our respective jobs despite the pain and sense of loss. And through this mutual struggle, we were closer than ever as a family. We had learned to rely on each other, and to varying degrees, rely on God during the worst of times.

"I believe God allows us to grieve as long as we need to," JM told me. "God grieves with us, and when He knows the time for grief is coming to an end, He moves in and draws us out of the valley."

Chapter Eleven
Summer, 2009
Sit

"Our Lord, our Lord, how majestic is your name in all the
earth! You have set your glory above the heavens. From
the lips of children and infants you have ordained praise
because your enemies, do silence the foe and the avenger."
Psalms 8:1-2

The pace slowed in the summer. Graduation had passed, school activities were over, the memorial was finished, and the scholarship had been organized and awarded. It gave us some time to catch our breath and reflect.

Becky and Kayla started the process of cleaning Kelsey's room. Her dirty clothes had laid there in her closet since September 2. It was an emotional task of fits and starts. Finally, they collected and cleaned enough of Kelsey's clothes to have two quilts made of them, which Kayla gave Becky and me as Christmas gifts.

By then, I was tired of being sad all the time. Grief wears on you. While the grief seemed to be not as intense, my subconscious must have been roiling, for I began having nightmares. I would wake up and be moaning, "No, no." Spurts of anger would still erupt. I would think of Kelsey and slam my fist on my desk or kick the air. It was like a reflex. It just seemed to suddenly pop out. Sometimes while riding my bicycle, I would start peddling at a sprint until I could not peddle any more, and I would coast to a stop in an asthmatic wheeze and heave.

In early July we took a family trip with the Howells to Myrtle Beach, South Carolina, where Becky's father, Eustace, lived. We had been to Myrtle Beach many times before, and I knew there would be a tug of memories. The long 1,500 mile trip east gave me much time to reflect and remember the many family trips down the same highway. The two days it took to reach the Atlantic had many Kelsey moments.

On the first night at the beach, I had another. As we stood on the balcony and watched people shoot fireworks into the sky from the beach, I remembered how Kelsey and I two years ago had watched the fireworks together. The sense of Kelsey was so strong I could almost smell her next to me.

Other memories: we ate at a seafood restaurant where Kayla and Kelsey had an argument two years before. It all flooded back to me. Meanwhile, Kayla continued to take photographs with an extra degree of care- the way Kelsey always did.

While we went to Myrtle Beach with the Howells, John Michael traveled to Macedonia on a mission trip under the direction of Randy Boyd. We had helped John Michael raise money for the trip and knew how important this was to him. The 6,000 mile trip took 36 hours, and he was without his luggage for three days. But that was nothing but a slight annoyance. "We were in a small room at Pastor Venco's in Cocani," he wrote me, "with an old drum set, an out-of-tune guitar, and six Macedonians that were absolutely on fire for the Lord. There were Macedonians, Hungarians, Albanians and Americans- four different languages being spoken all at the same time, yet all unified in praising the One True God. I finally got to experience the true church described in the Book of Acts- no luscious buildings, no expensive clothes; just genuine worshipping God in spirit and truth."

Every night they would travel to other towns in Macedonia, reaching out in prayer, dance, song, and skits in churches that were as old as the first century. "I was given the opportunity to speak at two of these events. I spoke about my life over the past year and how there was only one hope: Christ. Our lives are full of moments," he said, "and it is what we do with those moments that determine our destiny."

During the first week, he experienced an exorcism, in which he helped pray at the home. Then in the second week, while in Albania, he saw something even more amazing. They visited a house amidst the "gypsy slums" of an Albanian town, and in that house was a twelve-year old mute boy. His mother said the boy had never before uttered a single word. John Michael and the others prayed for the boy, asking Jesus to help the boy. "Open this boy's mouth," they prayed, "for Jesus died for him." Then they told the boy to say, "Jesus," and to everyone's utter surprise, he did. "Say it again," they said, and once more the boy said, "Jesus." And then on the third time, the boy yelled out, "Jesus!"

"It was one of the coolest things I had ever been a part of," John Michael told.

As he was returning home, he flew into Houston Intercontinental Airport. It so happened that Bec and I were flying to Iowa that evening, and we were also at Houston Intercontinental. As we waited in the terminal for our flight to Des Moines, up walked JM. It was a wonderful surprise. He told us of his experiences in Macedonia and Albania, and I could see in his eyes and hear in his voice the joy of the Lord.

While in Iowa, I noticed a change of heart in myself. Since Kelsey had died, a part of me did not care if I lived. After all, dying ended the pain and re-united me with Kelsey. As I said before, it was not a death wish; more of a life detachment. But as I visited my family and friends, I realized I was not ready to die. There was more life to be lived. I sensed God was not finished with me yet. I still wanted to get to heaven and see Kelsey. And now I realized I also wanted to get there to see God. But it would happen in God's time. And as I accepted that, a sense of peace started to grow inside me.

Despite all the traveling, "sit" was an important word to me in the summer of 2009. Randy Boyd, the missionary who led the Macedonian trip, and father of Bethany, one of the girls on the basketball team with the twins, had given me a copy of "Sit, Walk, Stand," by Watchman Nee[33]. The essential theme of this Nee work was that God was the active agent. The initial human task was to "sit" and let God work on him or her.

This ran antithetical to my nature. I wanted something to do. I thought my task was to seek God. Asking God to help with one's faith was a kind of cheating, a mooching, the lazy man's way to salvation. But Watchman Nee said in effect, "Be still and let God seek you." This was also consistent with what both John Michael and Pastor McMeans had told me.

Actually, this notion had already started making sense to me. I remember when reading *Mere Christianity*, C.S. Lewis had argued that true faith does not come until you try over and over again to obey God's law, and finally, after failure after failure, you realize you cannot do it on your own and must rely on God[34]. That becomes the moment of surrender.

One Wednesday night in D-team, I was saying (really complaining) that while I respected and feared God as the creator and judge, I did not love God- at least not enough. Austin Taylor suggested, "Let God love you." Simple, but profound. Later, IABC's assistant pastor, Mike Menasco, said in a prayer, "Let God invade us." I thought that was a really good way to say it. So after the flurry of the spring, summer became a time to sit; sit and let God invade and reveal.

About this time the song by Sanctus Real, "Whatever You're Doing," began to resonate. It began with "It's time for healing" and in the fall of 2008 I was not ready for that. Now I could feel myself moving towards that. Lines like "There's a wave crashing over me, all I can do is surrender" hit home with a particular power.

Meanwhile, Jeremy confided to me that he had many of the spiritual questions that once filled me. Initially, he had gone to church with Shannon, then quit. He went to IABC with us a few times. I encouraged him to attend church, but did not press him on it. I also gave him a copy of my manuscript *From Ayn to Awe*, telling him that I once had many similar questions.

I thought I had come to terms with the question of why. During the summer of 2009, I realized I had been premature. On the local news twin boys drowned in a local lake. Becky turned to me with a blank face and said, "They lost both of them." I spent the next day thinking of how easily that could have been us, that if the dump truck would have been just a foot to the left (a fraction of a second), Kayla would be dead, too.

My heart hurt for that family of twins. Why God? What is the purpose of this kind of tragedy and heartache? What good does it serve? I don't understand. I thought I did, but I guess I don't. Explain it to me please. How is Romans 8:28 ("all things work to the good") the truth?

So back to the question of why I rolled. Just as emotions spiraled and swirled, rolled and repeated, so did spiritual questions. Why such senseless tragedy? Why are we condemned to live in a world of so much uphill climbing? If You love us, then why do we have to endure so much pain? What is the purpose? *Is* there purpose to pain?

In the first eight to nine months after Kelsey was killed, I had believed that God's purpose in taking Kelsey was to shock us out of our spiritual complacency and spur us to growth. I did not like this, but accepted it, in part, because I knew that I needed to be kicked in my proverbial spiritual butt. I certainly did not believe the platitude that God needed another angel. At one point, I had even told JM that I thought the reason Kelsey died was God was coming for me. He wanted me to do something.

However, shortly after that pronouncement, I summarily rejected it. It stunk of arrogance, the "it's all about me" modern narcissism that I so detested. Furthermore, I could not live knowing that Kelsey had to die for my benefit. I was more important than Kelsey? Kelsey's life had less value? What kind of father could believe that?

This rejection was augmented by reading Doug Manning's book, *Don't Take My Grief Away from Me*. "God does not parlay one life against another. He does not take one life to punish another. He took the life He took because He thought it best for that life. Period.[35]"

So now what? If it was not to help me or others, why did Kelsey have to die? How could it be the best thing for Kelsey? I was more bewildered and lost than ever. I turned to the Bible. What did it say about this issue of God using tragedy to transform individuals or others?

I quickly discovered the Bible was fraught with personal tragedies and challenges initiated, or at least allowed, by God Himself. Abraham was commanded by God to kill his own son, Isaac, and then God withdrew the command at the last second. The entire book of Job was about God allowing Satan to utterly disrupt Job's life with a series of tragedies. At the behest of Satan,

God allowed Peter to be "sifted as wheat" on the night Jesus was arrested in Luke 22:31. The notes in the Zondervan NASB Study Bible for 2 Corinthians 1:9 states that "our weakness is precisely the opportunity for His power to be displayed."

So the Bible was stocked with examples of God using tragedy to develop trust. However, honestly at that point, I was asking why God even allowed the Devil to exist. God clearly had power over Satan; thus, Satan existed at the decision of God. I knew the intellectual answer, that sifting "removes the undesirable from desirable," as Pastor McMeans said from the pulpit. I had also heard that God allows bad to happen and then suffers along, too. And then there was the common adage that if Satan did not exist, God would have to create him. But at the moment, in the fog of Kelsey's death, none of that provided much solace. I was tired of the anguish and the evil. I was tired of being perpetually sad.

Rick Warren, in *The Purpose-Driven Life,* wrote that God uses us for His purpose. "If you want to know why you were placed on this planet, you must begin with God. You were born *by* his purpose and *for* his purpose.[36]" *His* purpose, not ours; which begged the question: what *was* His purpose in allowing Armor Asphalt to kill Kelsey? How was God, as stated in Romans 8:28, using it to make good?

I thought hard on this, prayed about it, and my mind kept gravitating to one of Kelsey's favorite verses: Proverbs 3:5: "Trust in the Lord with all your heart, and do not lean on your own understanding." Maybe that's it, I told myself. Maybe that's all we get to keep going on: we simply have to accept that some questions will not be answered- at least not on this side of the grave. By now you know me well enough to know that I was not at ease with that answer. I wanted to know.

In 2 Corinthians 12:7-9, Paul had some physical affliction described as a thorn in the flesh. Paul implored God to remove it. God refused. "My grace is sufficient for you." And then adds, "... for power is perfected in weakness." God did answer the prayer and the answer was "No." Sometimes that is all we get, and it is up to each of us to accept that and use it as best we can.

So what was left for us to do? The answer was obvious: trust. It wasn't easy then, and to be honest, it still is not for me. I don't trust easily. And whoever said "just trust," as if it was easy, was either naïve or not dealing with something of any depth or complexity.

I thought of the day I would enter heaven. I had a long list of questions, with the why question being the first of them. Then I thought about it some more. Would all those earthly questions simply evaporate in the presence of Jesus and God? Essentially, that was what happened to Job. All his questions and troubles immediately shrunk to insignificance in the face of God Almighty.

I remembered hearing Martin Luther King, Jr. say in the '60s that "undeserved suffering was redemptive." At the time I did not understand what that meant. Now Kelsey's undeserved killing forced me to focus on what that could mean. Was undeserved suffering redemptive? Was there purpose to the pain?

Not at first. Instead, it just seemed utterly unfair. Burying your child turns your life upside down. Kids are supposed to bury their parents, not the other way around. However, as time went on, I began to see that if you choose to love, then you risk the pain. Call it love's ante.

As I read the Bible and others, such as Watchman Nee, Viktor Frankl, and A.W Tozer[37], I came to understand that faith is a type of love. And if the price of love is pain, then it follows that faith does not absolve one from tragedy.

Did Kelsey deserve this? No.

Did we deserve this? No.

Then I asked a more important question: did Christ deserve the pain of the cross? Again, the answer was no. ...But He did it any way. Did we deserve grace, earn grace? No, but we got it any way.

So is there purpose to the pain? Is undeserved suffering redemptive? Yes, in Christ's finished work on the cross. Does that eliminate our anguish over Kelsey? No, we will still miss her. We will always miss her. If we did not want to risk this kind of grief, then we should not have had kids; we should not have dared to love. And life without love is only existence. So pain is part of it.

The good part? The best part? Christ opened a portal for all humanity. We will see Kelsey again. And it will be wonderful. In that I do trust.

In mid-July, after we returned from Myrtle Beach, I decided to write this book and started organizing notes. About that time,

I tried randomly opening the Bible to see where it led me, and I opened to Isaiah 61:1 "The spirit of God is upon me, because the Lord has anointed me to bring good news to the afflicted."

As I mentioned in the "On Authorship" at the beginning of the book, the original idea was for all of us to write our respective parts of each chapter. Accordingly, Becky wrote her part of chapter one, and then declared, "I can't do this." Nor, for the same reason, could she read the first few chapters and provide feedback. Even questions gently asked proved difficult.

We had a few arguments about it. "Then why did you tell me you wanted to do this?" I said once in disappointment.

"Cause I didn't think it would hurt so much!" she shot back.

I decided to accept and respect that, even though I thought a major part of the story would be missing. It took me a while to understand her resistance was about more than just the pain of reliving it. It was her way of coping. Just as she did not like Senior Night in basketball to be so much about Kelsey, she now did not want our daily routine to be about which chapter we were on. She simply was not ready for that.

Then over time, I began to also understand that her resistance was her way of expressing her love for me. She did not want to fight about it. She did not want to cry about it. There had been so much of that already.

In the spring of 2010, she was finally able to read some of the later chapters, which were about less searing events than that horrible first month or two. She answered my few questions and offered her memories and insights. But even that was difficult.

Each person deals with grief differently. That's the way it is. There's no "right way."

On one evening in late July, John Michael and Brian Valigura had finished working out at the Falls. As they drove home in Brian's car, they stopped at a red light. At this moment, JM heard God asking him if he was ready to move out of the valley he was in. "I pondered this question for several days," he told me. "At this point, I didn't know if I wanted to leave. It was all I had known for so long."

As he reflected and prayed, he asked himself if he was taking pride in being heartbroken. "I realized God was calling me to a new day. I had seen and felt God's loving hand and knew all of this happened for His glory and our ultimate justification. God leads us into things because He intends to be the hand that pulls us out."

God's hand was pulling on me, as well. A wonderful event occurred on July 22, 2009. It was not expected, which made it even more wonderful. After the accident, I had avoided that site. Then after the crosses went up, I would go by and check to make sure the wind had not blown anything over or weeds were not taking over. It was more of a care-taker mentality.

On July 22, as I drove to the office, I passed the accident site, and I said to myself: that is the place that Kelsey went to heaven. A big smile broke across my face. It was the first time that I could look at the two crosses as a place of positive, not just negative. It took me over ten months to come to that outlook.

Chapter Twelve

The Anniversary

*"Our fathers disciplined us for a little while as they
thought best; but God disciplines us for our good,
that we may share in his holiness. No discipline
seems pleasant at the time, but painful. Later on,
however, it produces a harvest of righteousness and
peace for those who have been trained by it."*
Hebrews 12:10-11

In August we concluded our dealings with Jimmy Hogan, owner of
Armor Asphalt, and Pedro Alcorte, the driver. We returned home,
and I went into Kelsey's room and sat on her bed. I looked up at
Proverbs 3:5 stenciled on her wall. Trust... does trust also mean
I'm supposed to forgive? I knew the answer before I finished the
question. Ronnie Quest, who had lost his daughter to drowning,
once told me, "At least you had someone to be mad at." However,
that also meant we had someone we had to forgive.

I thought of Viktor Frankl having to forgive the NAZIs. Then
I read pertinent Bible verses, including Luke 17:3-4. The Bible was
as clear as can be: forgiving was a command, not a suggestion. I
had a long way to go. I prayed for God's help.

Then another element arose. And it was personal.

John Michael had argued that we should not be vigorously
pursuing consequences for Jimmy Hogan and Pedro Alcorte. "It

was God's plan," he had said to me. "How do Jimmy Hogan and Pedro Alcorte feel knowing that they were a part of killing someone? I cried and prayed for them, knowing that they had to live the rest of their days with the fact that they had killed someone. Is that not punishment enough? Not once could I bring myself to be angry with them. Yes, in our society, people must pay for what they do. That's our way of life. That's how we think. But what did Jesus say to the men that were nailing Him to the cross? 'Father, please forgive them, for they know not what they do.' Christ said this of the men who *intentionally* killed Him. Jimmy Hogan and Pedro Alcorte did not intentionally killed Kelsey."

In contrast, Becky and I focused on direct legal accountability. While neither Becky nor I ever believed they intentionally killed Kelsey, it did not absolve them of appropriate responsibility for an accident that took a life. As Becky said, "They just can't cause a death and not pay for it in some way." As far as I was concerned, any guilt Hogan or Alcorte may have felt was an issue of their own consciences. The law was a separate matter. As was forgiveness.

Those were our respective views in August. Then it became more complicated. It turned out that Jimmy Hogan, owner of Armor Asphalt, was the second cousin of John Michael on his mother's side.

"At first," JM said, "I did not know that it was his company that owned the truck that killed Kelsey. I did not discover this fact until four or five months after the accident. When I learned that Armor Asphalt was owned by my second cousin, I asked myself what would Kelsey do? Would she be bitter towards Jimmy and Pedro, or would she see God's hand in all of this?"

Before he learned that it was his second cousin that owned the dump truck, JM had already resolved that he wanted to meet those responsible face-to-face and tell them he forgave them. "This was something the Lord had placed on my heart to do," he wrote me later, "and I knew I had to do it. From the moment everything happened on September 2, 2008, I never felt anger towards any man - not for one day; for the Lord had brought me to a place where I saw past man and saw God at the center of everything. He was still reigning on His mighty throne in the midst of this storm."

"I forgave everyone in this whole situation," John Michael

wrote me, "not because Kelsey did not mean as much to me, but because the Lord meant more. He alone is the alpha and omega. So forgiveness is not about saying, 'It's okay.' It's about saying, 'I love you.' You cannot forgive until you see the forgiveness that was given you by the Lord. Forgiveness comes through the hands of God."

In August Jimmy Hogan showed up at the Vestal home. John Michael walked up to Jimmy in the driveway and threw his arms around his 6'2" second cousin. "We talked about how good the Lord was," JM wrote me later. "And then Jimmy started crying like a little child on my shoulder. He kept saying over and over, 'I'm so sorry. I'm so sorry...' I answered, 'I forgive you and Pedro. I see God's hand in this, and I trust him. Our lives are not in the hands of anyone in this world, but in the mighty hands of God.'"

However, Becky and I had a different reaction when we learned that Hogan had visited the Vestals. My cynical nature smelled connivance and ulterior motives. The timing was too coincidental, and I took it to mean that Hogan was searching for a way to get John Michael to intervene on his behalf. While neither JM nor any one of his family ever did approach us, I believed Hogan was looking for some leverage.

John Michael had not told us before August that he was related to Jimmy Hogan. Was that because he was afraid to tell us? Was his advice on the matter influenced by his blood relation to Jimmy? Or did he honestly see the accident as part of God's plan?

I had some soul searching to do. Here was a young man that had come to mean a great deal to me. I respected and admired him. My daughter loved him. He loved my daughter. I loved John Michael. He loved me. Furthermore, he had lost just as much as we had. Indeed, he had lost a lifetime of tomorrows. And I knew he was in a bit of a tough position, as well.

John Michael and I discussed the situation, and he apologized for his second cousin. "It's not your fault," I told him. "Jimmy Hogan and Pedro Alcorte are responsible for their own individual actions." In my opinion, the creed of being your brother's keeper can be taken too far, and this was one of those times.

After much hard thought and prayer on the matter, I concluded John Michael was being honest and sincere: he truly believed the accident was part of God's plan. So did I for that matter.

However, I still believed in secular responsibility and attending consequences.

Of this episode, JM wrote, "This effected Thom and me. We had very different perspectives and disagreed about what should happen. Does that mean he was angry at me or I at him? By no means. In fact, I think it brought us closer together. We both believed God was using our grief to bring us closer to Him. And in the end, that was what really mattered."

The next time John Michael stopped by, we talked about another very personal subject: him dating again. I told him that needed to happen some day. When he was ready. Then I assured him we would not be offended or hurt. I reminded him of what I said to him the day after the accident: that we wanted to be invited to his wedding. Also, I added that the real tragedy would be if he was never able to go on and meet someone. Kelsey would not want him to be alone forever.

Sometime in mid-August, Alexandra Nanny came over, and I wrote the first check for the Kelsey Vines Memorial Scholarship. She showed us the scrapbook she had made of Kelsey. I was glad she was one of the first recipients of the scholarship. She is a class act. As is Taylor Langston, the other recipient. It was a pleasure writing those two checks.

Through the rest of August, the anniversary loomed over us like a dark cloud. Each day the pressure seemed to build as we slid towards September 2. School activities started up. The yearbook from the '08 -'09 school year arrived with a special dedication page to Kelsey written by Kayla.

For the first time in twenty years, we did not have a child in school. When the seniors took their photographs, I remembered the twins doing the same in anticipation of their senior year. One of my favorite photographs of Kelsey came on that August 2008 day. I remember thinking at the time the photograph was taken how beautiful she had become, how she had transformed from that gangly, awkward kid, and that John Michael and she had a wonderful future before them.

During late August, Kayla was extra reticent. Quiet. Subdued. I sensed she was having a tough time, not just because of the approaching anniversary, but because college was starting. For years Kelsey and she had anticipated going off to college. Now that that day had arrived, the hole where Kelsey was supposed to be arched larger than ever. "I was excited about starting this new journey in my life," Kayla wrote me later, "but I was also feeling guilty over being excited."

To my surprise, I discovered that I did not enjoy imagining Kayla going off to college, for when I let my mind conjure that up, it hurt. It was like Kelsey dying all over again.

As the days of August ran out, I began to wonder if the second year would be better than the first. I had read that for some it was the second year when the grip of grief held the strongest. How can that be? I asked myself. How could it be worse than this last year?

The anticipation of the anniversary kept building, and I wanted it to be over. We started getting cards and letters again, and many mentioned it in their conversations. Several asked if we were planning any ceremony, and I said that since everything from in the past year had been so public and in the news- the visitation, the funeral, the retiring of the jersey, the dedication of the memorial, and graduation, that we wanted something more low key and private. Just family.

Of course, John Michael was feeling the same burden that came with the anniversary. "It had been nearly a year since I had heard, seen, or felt Kels," he wrote me later, "and the thought of the anniversary did not allow me to get much sleep as I spent the night in Kelsey's room, just as I had on her birthday. I stayed up praying and reading the Bible. Most of the night consisted of the same question from me, and it was answered with the same answer from the Lord. 'Why did this happen, and what are you doing through it, Lord?' Answered by, 'I love you, John Michael, and my love for you is relentless and will accomplish exactly what it needs to.'"

. That night, while he was in Kelsey's room, I told him, "I realized something today. I realized that I still have three kids- two on earth, one in heaven." Until then, I had always believed that on an intellectual level, but something that I did not fully understand happened on September 1 that helped me to believe it in a deeper, more meaningful way. My knowledge and understanding went beyond the mind. I could feel that truth inside me. I don't know a better way to describe it than that. I could *feel* the truth. For someone so "left-brained" as me, this was an atypical reaction. I *knew* Kelsey was alive, and I would see her again. Someday.

On the morning of Wednesday, September 2, 2009, I had a dentist appointment. I had chipped a tooth because I grinded so badly at night. I had worn a mouth guard for decades, and after Kelsey died, the grind got worse. My dentist was Dr. Tracy Henson-McBee, a former student of mine from Meadow and a twin herself. When I came in that morning, I discovered that the entire staff was wearing red Kelsey t-shirts. I was very touched, but not surprised. Tracy had sent a card *every* week since the accident. It always gave a little pick-me-up.

After I left Dr. McBee's office, I stopped by Becky's office at North Elementary. I could see that she had been crying. I asked her if I needed to stay there with her. She said the other teachers were checking on her on a regular basis, and she was okay. More than ever I wanted this day to be over.

When I got to school, the Central Office staff had purchased a rose as a remembrance. I made the rounds in the office thanking everyone. It was hard to believe that it had been a year, and yet so much had happened that at times it seemed to be a lifetime ago.

At lunch I went over to the high school. I saw a few kids with red Kelsey t-shirts, and during passing period, I started to thank them for wearing the shirt. I had to quickly stop. I discovered that there were at least a hundred kids wearing the shirts, and I realized if I stopped them in the hall, I would cause a traffic jam. As far as I know, there was no concerted plan to wear the t-shirts. September 2 was a date burned into everyone's mind and memory.

"On the day of the anniversary," Kayla later wrote me, "I did not want to go to school. I found it difficult to focus in my classes, and I kept replaying the accident over and over in my mind. A few days before the anniversary, my Bible professor assigned a paper in which we were supposed to write about something that changed us and brought us to Christ. I thought the timing of this assignment was extremely ironic and yet appropriate. I knew this was a sign from God to remember that September 2 was not only a day to grieve, but a day to celebrate."

Likewise, John Michael was also on the LCU campus that day. "On September 2 I woke up and went to school as usual," John Michael told me, "except I wore my red Kelsey t-shirt with Matthew

139

6:34 on the front and number 15 on the back. Throughout the day, I looked around and wondered if anyone around me at school knew what had happened to me. I wondered if this day meant anything to them like it did me. Of course, this led me to more questions. Were there others who had lost someone they loved on this day, too? All day I didn't have a peace about September 2 and about what had happened exactly one year earlier. I began wondering, as I walked around campus, if I was where the Lord wanted me to be or if I hadn't allowed Him to accomplish all that He had wanted to do in me over that year.

"I was leaving my Anatomy and Physiology class and a classmate of mine saw my t-shirt and, "Who is Kelsey Vines?" I told him her story and about what that day meant to me. He then said, 'I am also dating a girl named Kelsey Vines.' This came as quite a shock."

It turned out that there were two Kelsey Vines: our Kelsey, and one from Austin, Texas, who was currently a student at BYU in Utah. JM's classmate was dating that Kelsey Vines. So here on the anniversary of the death of one Kelsey Vines, two young men came together in the same class at the same college over girls with the same name, girls who never knew each other.

"I knew this 'coincidence' was from the Lord," John Michael said. "I had been praying all September 2 for Him to do something amazing, to show me that He is still with me and for me. And sure enough He did. It blew me away, reassuring me that He is still with me and has not forgotten what He is taking me through and taking me to."

After school, Becky, Kayla, Jeremy and I met Todd, the Vestals, and the Vinsons at the crosses at the accident site. Someone had left a note at the site. When we arrived, JM was kneeing near the white marble cross. His manifest pain stung me, and I struggled not to get angry.

"Being at the accident site," Kayla told me, "hit me harder than I expected. All the memories flooded back and all the emotions I had held in came rushing out."

At 4:34 p.m., one year to the minute, I turned to the others and told them of what happened on July 22, how I had finally come to see this place in a positive light. Then I put my hand on the white marble veneer and said, "This cross represents our hope through the finished work of Jesus Christ." I remember John Michael gasping. I did not often say things that to John Michael were spiritually profound, and I think he was a bit surprised at it. Then I asked JM to lead us in prayer.

"This excited me," he later wrote, "because I knew the Lord had given me the strength to be the leader for all of us. I was still pondering the question of had the Lord done all that He had wanted to do in me over the last year? I had gone out to the accident site about thirty minutes earlier than everyone else to pray and to seek the Lord about this very subject. While I was standing before the cross, the Lord began to lay on my heart one of my favorite scriptures: Isaiah 55:10-11, which says *'As the rain and the snow come down from heaven, and do not return to it without watering the earth and making it bud and flourish, so that it yields seed for the sower and bread for the eater, so is my word that goes out from my mouth: It will not return to me empty, but will accomplish what I desire and achieve the purpose for which I sent it.'* This is a promise that the words He spoke to me a year ago did not come to me and return to Him void. When this verse came to my mind, a smile came across my face. In the midst of standing where my first true love met Jesus, and in the midst of that day itself, God was still able to make me smile.

"My dad was the first to come out to the accident site followed by the Vines, the rest of my family, and then the Vinsons. These were the people whom I cared about more than anyone. We had all been through the past year together. We had cried, smiled, and even laughed together over the last year. These were the people whom, over the last year, had hugged me when I needed to be hugged and whom I had cried many times on each of their shoulders.

"We circled around the cross that stood at the accident site, holding each other's hands and crying together. Thom asked me to pray. The Lord gave me words to speak. They just flowed out, and the Lord absolutely gave me a peace about that day and about Himself in my life. Even though we were all crying, I could feel the Lord comforting and holding me just as He had over the past year. I prayed for about five to ten minutes, and then it was over."

Alexandra Nanny saw all of us on the roadside and stopped, as did a few other people. She told us that she had put on her blog on My Space that there was a prayer vigil at the memorial at 8:00 p.m.

141

We thought it was just for the kids, so we decided not to attend. Kyle Edwards, Shanna, Kirstie and Kyle brought over Mexican food for supper. We looked forward to a quiet evening.

"We left there," John Michael later wrote, "and I headed to the Lubbock-Cooper Fellowship of Christian Athletes (FCA), which I had helped lead over the last year. They were having a special meeting tonight over at the Boyd's house to remember Kels and all that the Lord had done over the last year through it all. I came, and everyone there was wearing their Kelsey shirts, and even though it was 'the day', it felt comforting to see these kids whose lives had been transformed by the life of Jesus Christ that had lived in Kelsey.

"We talked and then began to sing some worship songs. Bethany Boyd, who had become one of Kelsey's best friends right before she died, got up and spoke. She spoke with strength in her voice that was from the Lord. She spoke of not letting the fire that started a year earlier die down.

"This struck me because, as I said earlier, God had asked me if I was ready to come out of this valley I was now in. I remember thinking throughout the summer if people were now moving on and if they had forgotten what happened on September 2. The thought of this angered me in a way. How could you move on from this, how could you forget? This event changed my life forever, and yet, people were forgetting about it and just moving on living their lives, as if nothing had happened? God reminded me once again though, that even if people who said their lives were changed forever had gone back to their normal ways, I hadn't. He had taken me on a year long journey of struggling and succeeding, doubting, yet trusting and losing, yet gaining everything I had ever needed. It was all about Him and me, not anything more or less. Intimacy with the Lord was the only thing that truly mattered. The past year had taught me that. And as I was sitting there listening to Bethany talk about the Lord, it reminded me of the love the Lord and I had shared over the last year. This love was the one and only reason I was able to be where I was."

At 7:30 Kayla called. People were starting to arrive at the memorial, and she suggested we had better get out there. We drove to the memorial, and two hundred people were there, including a television crew.

"To me it was a glorious site," JM wrote later. "This was the answer to my earlier question: had everyone forgotten about Kels and what September 2 had meant? The answer was no, and I hope that someday September 2 becomes a symbol for all of us to realize what Kelsey once told me, 'that life is short, and tomorrow is never guaranteed, but a life with Jesus Christ is.' So even those these days will be tough, we have to someday see the hand of God in these days, and realize that He has a plan, and it's been fulfilling itself since the beginning of time."

As usual, Alexandra served as the de facto master of ceremonies. Kayla thanked everyone for being there, and then handed the microphone to me. I pointed at the granite bench made by Sadler Monument, and said as important as the basketball on the bench was to Kelsey, it was the inscription of Matthew 6:34 on the side of the pedestal that was Kelsey's real focus. That was what she was about. Bethany Boyd related the story of how Kelsey had told her during the previous week that the Lord was going to do "something amazing" at LCHS. Alexandra and others told "goofy Kelsey" stories, including the red pepper story- which was the first time I had ever heard the tale. We all had that Irish wake that we did not have a year ago. It felt good. And I think for many the anniversary generated a sense of closure.

"We were there for about two or three hours," JM wrote, "talking about Kels, and just catching up with many people we hadn't seen in almost a year. It really built me up, and made the day feel so much better. I remembered many of Kelsey's friends coming up to me, and telling me that I changed her life, and through that I changed theirs, as well. These kinds of statements are the faith builders. The ones that God gives us every so often to remind us that this His plan is working, even though I had spent many nights over the last year asking God why, and are you really even doing anything in me, or even through me?

"I was one of the last few to leave the memorial, and I remember sitting on Kelsey's bench with my hand on the basketball, saying, 'God, I know You're still working, and I will keep going on this journey because You have kept me going this long.

"I went home that night with a sense of peace and excitement. I had a peace about what that last year had meant, and about what the new year ahead would bring. The excitement I had was about the future, and about trusting God more in my own personal life. Trusting that He was using me even though I was just a college student living what the world would say is a typical life. All the anticipation I had had for that day, and the anxiety had actually been for nothing. God had provided as He always had, and I made it through a day that a year earlier I had told myself that I couldn't make it through. Many days were still to come, but God was with me always and through the anniversary. All the things He did for me on this day, I saw His mighty hand even more so in my life."

Chapter Thirteen
Here We Are

"As the rain and the snow come down from heaven, and do not return it without watering the earth and making it bud and flourish, so that it yields seed from the sower and bread for the eater. So it is my word that goes out from my mouth: it will not return empty. But will accomplish what I desire and achieve the purpose for which I sent it."
Isaiah 55: 10-11

"After the anniversary, I felt a sense of peace I hadn't felt before," Kayla told me. "I knew Kelsey was better off, and that gave me a sense of comfort."

We were gratified that so many had spontaneously come out to show their love for Kels. But mostly what fed my own inner contentment was the deep conviction that, in the truest sense, Kelsey was alive- in a different dimension (that I did not really understand), was happier than any human on earth, and I would see her again. Several times a day I would think of that, and a wide smile would slide across my face. The song "There Will Be a Day" by Jeremy Camp captures that feeling perfectly[38].

However, despite a sense of peace about Kelsey, I was amazed and distressed how much grief still dominated every day during the second year. A daily grind of numbing heartache. While not as piercing, it was still very much present. It was more of a hollow, a hole rather than a sword or a spear. Kelsey was gone. Gone. That reality was the first thing I thought of in the morning and the last thing at night. Each day still seemed to bring a Kelsey moment. I concluded that I was sentenced to looking at life through "Kelsey glasses." I tried to see the time with Kelsey as a gift, but that ushered little solace, and most certainly did not erase the pain. I still longed to hug and hold my daughter. Grief, we discovered, was a lot like peeling an onion. There was layer upon layer, and each new layer produced some fresh juice to sting your eyes and attack your senses. You never get over losing a child. That's just the way it is.

In November April Ehlers told us that she chose number 15 as her basketball jersey at LCU. We enjoyed watching her play while wearing Kelsey's old number. Then just before Christmas, one of Kelsey's classmates left a street intersection sign near the marble bench in the memorial garden. One of the streets was "15th," and the other was "Kelsey." We did not even know there was a Kelsey Street in Lubbock County. We were going to return the sign to the City of Lubbock, but one of Lubbock-Cooper's police officers told us that the City would simply dispose of it. "You might as well keep it," he suggested, so we did. We attached it to the corner of our home in the back veranda. It was nice to know that Kelsey's classmates still thought of her and missed her, even if they were committing criminal acts to show it.

In late December Becky and I traveled to Michigan to visit Jason and his family. We spent most of the time at their log cabin home in northern Michigan, including New Year's Eve. I thought I was doing fine, but as the seconds ticked away on 2009, emotions started washing over me, just as they had a year earlier, and once more I was completely unprepared. Standing before a dying bonfire, I thrust out my arms, looked up at God, and asked "Why!?" The raw power of the moment surprised me. I thought I was past that kind of pain. Maybe we never get completely past it.

A few days later on the flight back to Dallas, I fell asleep. As I was napping, I realized Kelsey was dead. I awoke with a jerk. It was like discovering it all over again. It was horrible. By then, I had finished the first draft of this book. What both of these episodes showed me was that despite having written a book on my experience, there was a significant part of me that still denied that it happened. Denial died hard. And questions were never completely answered.

On January 14 Kayla gave Becky and me our belated Christmas gifts- the quilt made from Kelsey's clothes. It was touching. And yet, it hurt just a little to touch those clothes.

Later that night, while John Michael and I were discussing the writing of this book, something else happened that came as a surprise. As he was getting ready to leave, he paused and turned back towards Becky and me. He had a tentative, uncertain look in his eyes, which was not his normal demeanor. "There's something else I want to tell you about." Instinctively, I knew what he was about to tell us. He was dating a girl. She is "really nice," he said with a smile. And she had a burgeoning faith. Becky smiled. I smiled. Then he told us her name: Kelsey. He told us that he told her about Kelsey Renee, and she responded, "I hope she would approve of me." I smiled at John Michael and then added, "There's an expression that may be appropriate here: 'don't make her compete with a ghost.'"

Later, JM wrote me how he met this new Kelsey. "It was Friday, September 11, 2009, and I was at my brother's football game against Odessa Permian. I did not go to the game hoping to find someone to fall in love with. I saw this girl on the Monterey dance team standing on the bottom row. 'Wow, she's pretty,' I thought, and that sort of shocked me. I had not looked at another girl for over a year. I sat down, and I felt the Lord say, 'She needs me and you need her.' I asked my mom to find out her name, and when she told me it was Kelsey, it was a real shock.

"At the next football game, I introduced myself, and we talked for awhile. Then a couple of weeks later, we started dating. There was a part of me that was very hesitant to do this, but I felt the Lord calling me out of the valley. When the Lord initiates something in your life, there is no denying it. If we cannot see the hand that took us into the valley, we will not be able to see the hand that led us out. They are one in the same."

I was not shocked that JM was dating another girl. I was not even shocked that her name was Kelsey, or that her dad's name was Tom, although that did seem a little coincidental, almost to the point of being eery. What I was shocked by was my reaction.

That JM was dating again was bound to happen. It had to

come. It needed to come. The tragedy would be if it did not come. Both Becky and I were happy for him.

But that was my head talking. My heart whispered something else. "He's moving on. ...He's abandoning our Kelsey." And even though my head said, "Nonsense, you are being irrational," and "You're acting like a hypocrite" (after what I said to him on September 3 and in the following August), my heart felt a different reality. In some convoluted way, it felt as if Kelsey was dying just a little bit more. Of course, that is absurd, but I felt it anyway.

I cried that night. In pain and in joy. In pain for myself and my family. In joy for Kelsey living in the light of heaven. And in joy for John Michael finding his way through the darkness. With God's help. By His grace.

But there was one other thing that really shocked me. I was shocked to discover how much I had relied on John Michael. I suddenly recognized that I relied on him to keep a sense of Kelsey alive. When he was near, she was near. He was a physical connection, a walking reminder. But now as he drew away, as he had to, it was like losing a part of Kelsey.

Furthermore, I realized how much I had leaned on him for spiritual guidance. He was one of my primary spiritual teachers, just as he had been with Kelsey. And suddenly, that was in danger of slipping away, as if the raft we were both on had cracked in two, and the current took him one direction and I another. I was dismayed at my reaction, and chastised myself: I'm not nearly as strong as I thought I was.

However, I also learned that the sense of reliance was mutual. "Your growth is what often kept me going," he told me after January 14. "You humbled yourself before God, and in that more than anything else, I saw the working hand of God."

Seared by loss, molded by God, John Michael and I grew together in head and heart. We reached across our mutual pain and gave each other hope.

I don't make New Year's resolutions. I have goals instead. Some long-term, some short. On New Year's Day 2010, I asked myself what did I want to do with the rest of my life. It took me several weeks for the answer to coalesce in my mind.

There were actually many answers. Take care of my family. Finish my school administration career. Maintain a modicum of health, with an emphasis on minimizing pain. Maybe travel some. Even take a divinity course at Harvard.

Then through the murky waters of my future, two goblets of oil rose to the top and spread across the surface, producing a sheen that reflected back to me. Above all, I wanted my remaining days to be about loving and serving God. The other thing? Wait until I got to see Kelsey again.

What did not seem to matter as much were health issues. Relieve pain? Yes, I wanted to avoid pain. Live longer? Not as important. After all, that would just prolong the time when I got to see Kelsey again.

So a residue of apathy still ran in my veins. I often caught myself saying, "It's just…" "It's just food," I would say, when someone fixated on some new restaurant. "It's just clothes," when someone dreamed of wearing the latest fashion. "It's just a car." "It's just a piece of furniture." "It's just…"

It was not that I didn't care for life. It was just that I cared more about the after-life. I realized that if I ever have grandchildren, I will probably change and want to see them grow up.

Likewise, the apathy manifested in changing priorities. I would see a photograph of me before the accident and realize that I had aged three years in that one. Then I would shrug and say, "Oh, well." However, when I develop some serious illness and actually face mortality, then we will see just how much of a hypocrite I am.

The detachment and apathy took a toll on my career, as well. For thirteen years, I had served as the Assistant Superintendent and then Deputy Superintendent of Lubbock-Cooper ISD under Superintendent Pat Henderson. All during this tenure, I had studied and prepared to one day become the Superintendent after Pat retired. However, after Kelsey died, I simply did not have that kind of focus or drive any more. My priorities had changed. I knew that with that outlook, I did not need to become the Superintendent. In January 2010, I told Pat I would complete the bond construction and then retire.

Thus, the material world and the physical body do not have the hold on me that it used to. They are not real because they are not lasting. What is? The answer is clear. God was everlasting. It is God that is real.

I spent decades racked by doubt. Doubt is not necessarily a bad thing if it becomes the platform to questioning and seeking, to letting God reveal Himself. My faith actually deepened as a result of wrestling with my doubts. God likes honest questions and dialogue. Job doubted and complained- complained bitterly; but he talked *to* God, not *of* God.

And while I have answered many questions and resolved many issues, some doubt still remains. And I suspect there always will be some. The difference is that I am now okay carrying some doubt. I don't have to know every answer to every question. I trust God will reveal His plan on His schedule.

For instance, I still have doubts about Biblical inerrancy. Are Genesis 1 and 2 accurate or allegory? In November 2009, I purchased *The Language of God* by Francis Collins, the head scientist of the human genome project, and a Christian believer[39]. Collins noted that the genome project was an "occasion to worship." He believes creation was God-initiated, and God simply used evolution as His pre-determined method.

But what about the Fall? If there was no actual Adam, if there was no original sin, no fall from innocence into sin, then there was no need for a savior. Collins quoted C.S. Lewis, who believed Genesis 1 and 2 were allegory, as well, but still believed there was a Fall. "...Sooner or later they fell. Someone or something whispered they could become as gods..."[40]

"Sooner or later? Someone or something?" Not a very satisfying answer. But again, the difference now is that I accept that not all questions will be answered- at least not on this side of the grave. I accept that while maybe some of the Bible is allegory, the main message is not. God created the universe *somehow*. I believe in the first four words of the Bible: "In the beginning God..." How is not nearly as important to me as who. I also believe that Jesus is the Christ. He did save me and everyone else. It is up to us to accept that gift. If the Bible is not 100% inerrant in the literal sense, that does not disqualify its basic, essential truth.

Why can I now accept this less than pure ideological, theological stance? Because I trust God. In fact, I now can look at unanswered questions as an opportunity to trust. That is quite a change for me. A wonderful change. Nothing less than a blessing.

Upon what do I base this trust?

Simple. I know He loves us. This seems simple and almost matter-of-fact, but it is not. In fact, it is quite profound and utterly important. He *loves* us. He wants the best for us, just as I want the best for my family. We are His family. Tim Watson's "Just remember that God loves you" is as pertinent today as it was then, maybe more so.

How do I know He loves us? How am I convinced of this despite the fact He let my daughter die? The answer lies in asking why were we put here. Why did God create us? Why would He go to all the trouble? And the answer: God wants to love and be loved by people who have free choice to decide. And correspondingly, He has sorrow and anger when we choose not to meet His love with our love. The desire for love is one of our most basic of human desires and needs. And from where did we get that? From the God in whose image we were made.

Could I be wrong about the God of love? Could the opposite be true? God hates us? He put us here to as part of some sadistic scheme for His amusement? Voltaire said, "God is a comedian playing to an audience afraid to laugh."[41] Could that be true?

I don't think so. He eventually would tire of that pointless exercise and rid Himself of us. What would be the point of such a creation? The purpose? Why would we be born to simply suffer and die? If that was the case, then some of the existentialists would be right, and we are simply enduring a purposeless existence.

I believe God does not move without purpose. Consequentially, our life does have purpose. What is that purpose? He created us to love, and be loved. Forever.

On the evening of March 1, 2010, I texted JM: "Tomorrow will be 18 months." He texted back a long message, that included "Has God missed a day in the past 442 days of loving you?"

"I still do not know the why," I responded, "but I trust the how. God loves us. How can we then not love Him?"

However, being loved by God does not mean we will be free of trial and travail. Proverbs 3:12 and Hebrews 12:6 teaches us that God chastens and disciplines those He loves.

I used to see God as some remote statue- like being hidden behind a veil that we were not supposed to approach, like the Wizard of Oz behind the curtain. Now I see that He is a personal God, who approaches us, seeks us, invades us. I used to believe that I could think my way to God. It was vanity. It was ignorance. It was arrogance. It was fear of giving up control. God wants a relationship, not an associate. He wants a loving servant, not just an observant student. He wants us to *rely* on Him, and what losing Kelsey has taught me is that He will *force* us to rely on Him as a means of drawing us closer.

To rely on something, you have to trust. Inevitably, trusting God comes down to accepting God's outcome, not insisting on a particular result. His goals are our goals. And He will create circumstances that will require us to rely on Him. Inevitably, my family and I look upon Kelsey's death as that kind of circumstance.

So then I had to ask myself a question that could no longer be ignored: did I trust God and His plan enough to forgive Jimmy Hogan and Pedro Alcorte? Could I forgive the people that took our Kelsey from us?

This was *tough*. This was not some intellectual exercise in some seminary debate. This was personal.

One day in the autumn of 2009, I saw on a street a dump truck owned by Armor Asphalt. I wanted to yell at it: don't you know what your callousness has done? You took a beautiful life and scarred the rest of us for the rest of our lives. For months, I got a sense of satisfaction by telling myself that one day Armor and Alcorte would get theirs.

As time went on, I realized I had to get past this. I had to let it go. Part of the reason it was hard to let it go was because, at times, hating felt good. It felt right. I bathed myself in justified anger. However, gradually over time I saw my self-righteous ire was also self-centered and counter-productive. It was a road block. I knew I had to let it go. I had to forgive. Just like Viktor Frankl with his NAZI persecutors, if I were to go on, I had to forgive. I had to trust God and His purpose even though I did not understand it. His love had to supersede my hate and bitterness.

I asked myself: will God forgive Jimmy Hogan and Pedro Alcorte? Is this a trick question? All they have to do is sincerely ask for it, which I would bet they already have.

So now it was up to me. Could I give what I have already received? God forgave me and everybody else when none of us deserved it. Pastor McMeans said, "Before we can forgive, we must first receive forgiveness from Jesus."

Then I discovered that forgiving is not a letting go, at least not at first; rather, it is a re-living, a re-opening of wounds, a taking on, a new suffering. That is why it is so easy to ignore the need to forgive and just go on hating.

Thus, I did not need to confront Hogan and Alcorte. Instead, I needed to confront myself. And as I did, I felt the bitterness and rage subside within me. I forgave Jimmy Hogan and Pedro Alcorte. God's love trumped man's hatred. That does not mean they did not do anything wrong. It just means I forgive them for their mistakes.

However, over time I was shown that forgiveness is a journey and process in itself. For instance, in the summer of 2010, Quaker Street was being widened about a quarter of a mile from my home. One of the contractors? You guessed it: Armor Asphalt. Every morning as I drove to work, I had to look at their dump trucks with Armor Asphalt painted on the side. Each time I had to tell myself: let it go.

Over time, I realized there was one other thing to do. Even though I had forgiven them in my heart, it did not seem complete. Instinctively, I knew I had to express my forgiveness to Hogan and Alcorte. I thought on this for several weeks, and finally on October 20, 2010, I drove to the offices of Armor Asphalt and asked to see Jimmy Hogan. He was out on jobs. I left a message for him to call, which he did the following day. I told him I had prayed on it, that we knew the wreck was never intentional, and we had forgiven. "You don't know how much this means to me," he said several times. I could hear the relief in his voice.

When I hung up, it felt good. It felt right. That does not mean it was not hard, but the bottom line here is this: we were forgiven through Christ's sacrifice on the cross. And just as we were forgiven, we must forgive.

Then on Wednesday, October 27, Jimmy and I met in my office at school. He sat down across from me, and suddenly I found I could not look at him. I had forgiven him in my mind. I had forgiven him in my heart. I had even expressed those words to him over the phone. But actually seeing him proved more difficult than I had anticipated. I took a deep breath, looked up at him, and told him of our forgiveness. We talked for nearly an hour, each shedding tears, while sharing our perspectives and our faiths. When Jimmy left, I was more satisfied than ever I had made the overture to him.

A few hours later, I drove to the gravesite to "tell" Kelsey. I sat down on the grass beside her grave and broke down.

That afternoon I wrote a letter to Pedro Alcorte expressing our forgiveness. It had been 785 days since Kelsey died.

I do not know why God permitted the pin in the steering box of the dump truck to snap, sending the truck veering left into the other lane. I do not understand how that fit God's plan. But here's the main point: while I do not understand it, *I trust God.* No longer do I lean on my own understanding. Kelsey's verse of Proverbs 3:5 is something more than some words painted on a wall. It's personal. It has special meaning.

Were we being punished? No, Christ paid for our sins. He took on all our punishment. As odd as it sounds, I now know that on September 2 we were being loved. If you had told me that on that day, I would have probably kicked you in the shins or worse. I still don't understand it all, but now accept that I don't have to. I don't understand how Kelsey's death fits God's greater purpose. *But it did.* Again, how do I know this? Because God loves us.

God used Kelsey and is using us for His purpose. We modern-day Americans are so narcissistic that we want God for our purposes, and that's not how it works. We did not have a choice about September 2. For some reason, we were chosen by God to go through this. Only God knows why we were chosen for this.

However, while we did not have a choice about September 2, we did have a choice about September 3 and 4 and... We had a choice in how we reacted. I cannot say that I am glad that we went through this. That said, I now see that in a real way this experience has been a gift from God. As tough as it has been, it has forced all of us to confront what we really value. I recognize that the sadness, anger, and questioning channeled us down a road that brought us closer to God. Priorities were changed. Insight was gained. I recognize now that tragedy is one of the ways (maybe the main way) that God works us towards someday being perfected in heaven.

Discerning God's plan can be folly and arrogance, but if I *had* to offer a guess at why the events unfolded as they did, I would project the following. God brought Kelsey and John Michael together so her faith could flower. She, in turn, became a wonderful witness for Christ- in her life and in her death, which impacted many and transformed some, particularly me. Then John Michael and I wrote this book in an effort to help others with similar questions and pain. Perhaps that set of dominoes is too neat. Maybe that chain of events is wishful thinking, a vain hope to find meaning out of misery. I stipulate that my interpretation could be wrong ... but, obviously, I don't think so.

This is not to say that the grief is over. It will never be completely over. For the rest of our lives there will be a hole where Kelsey is supposed to be. What would she have become? What would our grandchildren look like?

The smartest individual in our D-team is Eric Davis, called Elmo by everyone. He is studying nuclear physics- enough said. Once while discussing himself, he noted that there is a certain pride to misery. That caught my attention. I was guilty of that, too. At times it was like a badge of honor. See how we held up. Or was it? See how we don't want to completely give it up. As I mentioned before, at times grief was a companion; a crutch like a drug is a crutch.

In some ways, I feel these past two years has been our Churchillian moment, our finest hour. We conducted ourselves in a time of travail with a modicum of courage and dignity. Then at other times, the legacy is simply one of bitterness, and an overwhelming sense of loss. I suspect that dichotomy will endure the rest of our lives.

It has been gratifying to see Kayla's faith grow in crisis. And I trust that God, in His time, will answer Jeremy's questions.

I began asking myself if I was ready to move on. If so, does that mean I'm callous? Or if I'm not ready does that mean I'm selfish and weak? The grief has lost some of its sting mainly because the joy I have found in Christ has spread a wonderful balm on my anguish. And as I grew within Christ's loving cocoon, I noticed that the rage inside me (that I had long before Kelsey died) slowly subsided, like the coals in a campfire slowly dying.

When did grief hit rock bottom? I'm not sure. But I know I

155

turned a significant corner on that July day that I could see the accident site as the place Kelsey went to heaven.

Despite that, denial refuses to completely die. Every time I see JM pull up in his pick-up, a flicker goes through the back of my mind: he's here to pick up Kels.

I aged three years in that one, and as tough as it was, I know that if we had any doubts about Kelsey being in heaven, or we had been in a different community, just how much tougher it would have been. Words do not fully describe the depth of our gratitude. I still break into a smile when I see a car with a Kelsey sticker on their back window, or a student wearing a Kelsey t-shirt at school, or a yellow or blue Kelsey bracelet.

Can it happen again? Can tragedy strike twice? Unfortunately, the answer is yes. There are no guarantees, no quota on pain. Does this scare me? Right down to my socks.

As I contemplated this, I finally realized what trust is. Trust is knowing that God will take care of us in the *long*-run. In the short-run (i.e. this side of the grave) we will be subject to tragedy and transgression, travail and trial. Adversity is part and parcel of our earthly lives. Trust is about submitting, even though we don't know how it is going to turn out. Trust is nothing but an act of courage. And love.

So is this finally the "new normal?" I don't know. Maybe all new normal really means is that you keep growing. I do know that grief dies from the outside in. The first to let go are the associates and acquaintances, then friends and relatives, and finally, family-and we all know that we never truly, completely let it go. It will be with us for the rest of our lives. But so will God. ...And for a whole lot longer.

The time since September 2 has been the most horrible and most wonderful time of my life. The horrible part is obvious. The wonderful part is the joy I have found in Christ, at which, like C.S. Lewis, I am positively surprised. I learned that joy is not the product of a set of circumstances, but comes through a relationship with Christ. It comes from trusting.

"I remember my mom saying," JM told me, "that if nothing else happens, what has happened in Thom's life is the biggest blessing through this tragedy." Kelsey always prayed that I would find a personal relationship with Christ, not just an intellectual one. I did, and in so doing, found a sense of peace that I never had before.

Often one does not understand how far one has come until they look back. I realized the length of my journey when JM read *From Ayn to Awe* and made notes. As I read those notes, I realized that *From Ayn to Awe* was now a defunct book. That person no longer existed. I had moved far beyond it. The trials and travails of losing Kelsey had served as the vehicle to transport me to a certain wisdom and a deeper faith. I am more compassionate and less self-absorbed. God had, indeed, used my weakness, and filled it with His strength.

Do I wish that we had not gone through this? Obviously. Indeed, there is still an element of shame and guilt that it took this to shake me out of my complacency. That said, it has been a time of tremendous personal growth, forced as it was, painful as it is. I was forced to confront whether I really trusted God.

The Bible repeatedly shows that people tested with undeserved trials and tragedies grow in wisdom because of their struggle. It really does build character. I now understand on a deeper level the love of Christ: he *chose* to suffer for our benefit. That level of sacrifice should humble us all.

What did I learn from this searing journey? I learned to be content because I am loved. And how can one not love someone who loves you? However, being content is not the same as being happy. I doubt I will ever again be able to truly think of myself as happy. To a significant degree, my life on this earth has been permanently ruined. And while I no longer yearn for death, neither do I fear it. There is certain liberation in that.

Grief is relentless, a daily challenge. It has become part of me and I accept that. In fact, the only thing that really gets under my skin any more is when I get the sense from someone else that they think we should be over our grief. You can almost hear they want to say: are you still stuck in this?

I accept that grief is the new normal. How can that be? Because I also know that my next life will be wonderful beyond description. And Kelsey will be right there beside me.

During my deistic days, I longed for two things: clarity and joy. I now have the clarity that comes from knowing the greatest truth of the universe: Jesus is the Christ. And I know that one day I will experience a thrust of joy as I enter heaven. Thus, an inner peace has settled in my mind and soul. I am forgiven, and I can forgive.

We, of course, were not the first to lose a loved one, and unfortunately, we will not be the last. The purpose of this book has been to help others with the grieving process, and the particular challenge of trusting God in the face of tragedy, but as I come to the end, I realize it is I that has been helped the most.

This book is not meant to eliminate grief. Nothing can do that. I pray we will help some family get through it just a little bit more easily, and maintain their trust in the Lord- or maybe develop a trust where it was not.

On the morning of March 2, 2010, I walked into Kelsey's room before I left for school. I sat down on Kelsey's bed, as I had so many times before. It's been a year and a half, I told myself. So much had happened, and yet it seemed like yesterday. I looked up at Proverbs 3:5 on her wall. I thought of Kels and the legacy she had left, and a smile broke across my face.

Later that month over spring break, I had some time to reflect on how I could honor Kelsey, and I concluded that one of those ways was to keep going, keeping plodding on. I told Pat that I probably would not retire in 2011, that I would take it a year at a time. Losing Kelsey has taught me not to plan beyond that, not get too far ahead of myself. Nothing is guaranteed to us.

On April 7, 2010, the twin's twentieth birthday, fifty-six people, mostly classmates, wished Kels Happy Birthday on her face book site. It was a very heart warming experience.

In May, 2011, we awarded the second Kelsey scholarship to Bethany Boyd and Tonya Becker. That summer, Bethany and Alexandra Nanny traveled to the Czech Republic on a mission trip. Afterwards, each related how they told the kids in the Czech Republic of Kelsey's story, and how it resonated with them. Alexandra, in particular, told of how in the days before September 2, Kelsey had told Alexandra that she wanted to "take the next step" with the Lord. Alexandra told these kids, that despite the obvious pain and shock after the accident, "I couldn't wipe the smile off my face" when I thought of Kelsey with the Lord. Many of these Czech kids were atheists, and Alexandra said many seeds were planted that day. For us, of course, it was heartwarming to see Kelsey still being a witness for Christ.

Also, during the summer of 2010, close friend and classmate, Katie Heinrich, while giving her retiring speech as a state FFA officer, talked of Kelsey. She talked of beauty, and how God's beauty is often misunderstood. She then told the story of Kelsey. "God's beauty," Katie said, "comes out during the heartbreak and hurt. ...Sometimes, the beauty is so deep it pierces us."

During October, 2010, John Michael came over to discuss the publishing of this book. With him he brought Kelsey's cell phone and diary that we had given him shortly after her death. The cell phone number, of course, had long been disabled. That night, after he left, I paged through the diary. I found strands of Kelsey's hair stuck between the pages. I caressed them with my fingers, then lifted them to my nose, and brushed them against my face. For just a second I was transported back.

Two recurring themes protruded from her writings: her love of JM, and her love of Jesus Christ. On August 26, with just seven days left on this earth, she wrote, "This year has been amazing. My life has been transformed. I love you, God, so much."

On September 1, her last full day of life, she quoted Mark 10:21: "Go sell everything you have, and give it to the poor and you will have treasure in heaven. Then come follow me." After that, she wrote, "God sometimes wants us to let go of what we truly love. ...Now all I can do is <u>grow</u> <u>in</u> <u>Christ</u>."

In late January, 2011, as I was proofing the galleys for this book, I received a gift. A gift from God, no less. It came unexpectedly, without wrapping or announcement. It was not a singular event, but a process; for indeed, I had glimpsed it before- a flicker here, an inkling there. But I never believed it would truly become part of the new normal, something I could count on as daily companion. The gift? A slow, but steady realization that Kelsey had been God's gift to us. A gift that lasted eighteen years. A gift that we would receive again when we were joined once more in heaven. A great peace came over me, and a smile slid across my face. While walking the dogs, I said a prayer of thanksgiving.

This does not mean an end to grief. That will only come with my last breath. But it does mean that hope wells within me, and a subtle, but sure joy flows through me.

The story of grief is one that slowly fades. In a Hollywood script there might be some dramatic ending, but in real life it is more subtle. There comes a quiet acceptance of the new normal. It's not a "moving on." Rather, it is more of a growing with, accepting of. We now know we will never "get over it." It will be part of our core experience for the rest of our lives. So we will be without Kelsey for some time, decades probably, but then we'll be together again. Forever. And then the time apart will seem like a flicker across the breadth of eternity.

When we grieve, we catch a glimpse of God for that is how He feels towards us every day. Because He loves us, He suffers, too. Christ cried for Kelsey right along side of us, and He walked with us through the dark days afterwards. Christ is the source of our strength and our peace. On Him we can rely.

So can you trust God when the absolutely worst thing happens?

Absolutely.

> *"You [Satan] intended to harm me, but God*
> *intended it for good to accomplish what is now*
> *being done, the saving of many lives."*
> **Genesis 50:20**

Epilogue

By Shelley Vestal (JM's mom)

I was blessed to have sweet Kelsey Renee in my life as she dated John Michael, my son for 11 months. She brought joy into all our lives. On September 2, 2008, our world was rocked to the very core, but it also took us on a journey of hope, trust, and faith.

Hope is what I most learned from Kelsey's death. Hope that God's purpose for our life is so huge. Hope that life does go on. Hope that His love for us is greater than we could ever imagine, and that one day we will go home to be with Him. Trust that He will carry us through no matter what and faith in knowing that God's love is never ending. Faith that God's love had set Kelsey free, and she knew it.

Kelsey lived her life as if each day were her last. She made sure everyone around her knew each day how much she loved them. When I first met her, she always had a smile and just loved life, but as her relationship with the Lord grew, she not only was happy, but she had hope! She knew that the Lord had made her whole, and she wanted everyone to have what she had. She had truly found her soul mate, not with my son John Michael, but with her Lord! There is no doubt in my mind that the Lord brought Kelsey into John Michael's life and that their love and her death have made him who he is today.

I truly could go on for hours about the many memories I have of Kelsey. I will treasure each one of them forever! One gift that she left us all is her photographs. All the many pictures she took have a little piece of her in them. They are like little footprints of her life she left behind for us to have. I will forever be grateful for having Kelsey in my life!

Kelsey's life and death have forever changed the lives of the people who loved her and knew her. When you think of her spirit, you cannot help but smile and have hope. When Kelsey left this world that September afternoon, she truly changed a community. She made many re-analyze their life and what it truly stood for. In any death, it seems impossible to see anything good come out of it, but through the months that followed, the Lord kept telling me over and over that: "When Kelsey left this earth to be with Me, she took that part of her father's heart that was hardened with her, and carried it to Me and I will make him whole." To me, this is the ultimate gift of love.

One of her favorite songs was "Hope Now" by Addison Road.[42] Every time I hear this song, I feel as if she is sitting right beside me singing along. It touches my soul. Here are the words:

"If everything comes down to love
Then just what am I afraid of
When I call out Your name
Something inside awakes in my soul
How quickly I forget I'm Yours

I'm not my own
I've been carried by You
All my life
Everything rides on hope now
Everything rides on faith somehow
When the world has broken me down
Your love sets me free

When my life is like a storm
Rising waters all I want is the shore
You say I'll be ok
Make it through the rain
You are my shelter from the storm

Everything rides on hope now
Everything rides on faith somehow
When the world has broken me down
Your love sets me free
You've become my hearts desires
I will sing Your praises higher
Your love sets me free."

As hard as it is to say, our sweet Kelsey Renee is home and that is all the hope I need! I love you sweet girl, and I thank you for loving me.

Shelley

Matthew 6:34
"So do not worry about tomorrow; for tomorrow will care for itself."

Endnotes

Chapter One

1 Mat Kearney, *Closer to Love*, City of Black and White, Aware/
Columbia, [2009], compact disc.

Chapter Three

2 Ayn Rand, *The Virtue of Selfishness* (New York: The New
American Library, 1961)

3 Julie Gold, *From a Distance*, Some People's Lives by Bette
Midler, Atlantic Records 7567-84888-4, [1990], compact
disc.

4 C.S. Lewis, *Mere Christianity* (Glasgow?: Fount Paperbacks,
1977).

5 Josh McDowell, *More Than a Carpenter* (Wheaton, IL: Living
Books, 1977), 60-71.

Chapter Five

6 Don Felder, Don Henley, Glenn Frey, *Hotel California*, Hotel
California by The Eagles, Asylum 45286 [1976], vinyl LP.

7 Randy Newman, *Feels Like Home*, What If It All Means Something by Chantel Kreviazuk, Columbia [2008], compact disc.

Chapter Six

8 Nichole Nordeman, *Legacy*, Woven & Spun, Sparrow, [2002],
compact disc.

Chapter Seven

9 Roger Nichols-Paul Williams, *We've Only Just Begun*, Close
to You by the Carpenters, A&M Records1217, [1970], LP.

10 Louie Giglio, Mat Maher, Jesse Reeves, Jesse Tomlin, Chris
Tomlin, *I Will Rise*, Hello Love, performed by Chris Tomlin,
EMI, [2008], compact disc.

Chapter Eight

11 Doug Manning, *Don't take my grief away from me*, (Oklahoma City, OK: In-sight Books, Inc., 1979).

12 Dylan Thomas, "Do not go gentle into that good night" in Literature: an introduction to fiction, poetry and drama, 2nd edition, edited by X.J. Kennedy (Boston: Little, Brown and Company, 1979), p. 579, line 1.

13 Don Piper with Cecil Murphey, *90 Minutes in Heaven* (Grand Rapids, MI: Revell, 2004).

14 Jim Wetherbe, *Faith Logic: Getting online with God* (Houston: Mead Publishing, 2007).

15 William Young, *The Shack* (Newbury Park, CA: Windblown Media, 2007).

16 Jeremy Camp, Jeremy Thomas, *There Will Be A Day*, Speaking Louder Than Before by Jeremy Camp, BEC Recordings, 2008, compact disc.

17 How Great is our God, dir. unknown, perf. Louie Giglio, DVD, Christian Cinema.com, 2007.

18 Brandon Heath, *Wait and See*, What If We, Sony BMG, [2008], compact disc.

19 Brandon Heath, *Wait and See*, What If We, Sony BMG, [2008], compact disc.

20 Dan Gartley, Mark Graalman, Matt Hammitt, Peter Prevost, Chris Rohman, *Whatever you're doing (something heavenly)*, We Need Each Other by Sanctus Real, Sparrows, [2008], compact disc

Chapter Nine

21 http://www.tameri.com/CSW/exist/dostoevsky.shtml. An article on Fyodor Dostoevsky's belief that suffering is part of the meaning of our life.

22 Tim Folger, "A Universe Built For Us", Discover Magazine (Dec, 2008).

23 Rick Warren, *The Purpose Driven Life* (Grand Rapids, MI: Zondervan, 2002).

24 Watchman Nee, *The Normal Christian Life* (Bombay, India, Gospel Literature Service, 1957).

25 C.S. Lewis, *Surprised by Joy: The Shape of My Early Life* (London: Harcourt, 1955).

26 John Mark McMillan, *How He Loves Us*, We Cry Out, Jesus Culture Music, [2007], compact disc

Chapter Ten
27 <u>The Passion of the Christ</u>, dir. Mel Gibson, perf. James Caviesel, DVD, Icon Productions, 2004.
28 <u>Saving Private Ryan,</u> dir. Steven Speilberg, perf. Tom Hanks, DVD, DreamWorks, 1998.
29 Deborah Brevoort, "The Women of Lockerbie", Dramatists Play Service, Inc., 2001.
30 Bart Ehrman, *Jesus, Interrupted* (New York: Harper One, 2009).
31 <u>Expelled: No intelligence allowed</u>, dir. Nathan Frankowski, perf. Ben Stein, DVD, Rocky Mountain Pictures,2008.
32 Viktor Frankel, *Man's Search for Meaning: An Introduction to Logotherapy* (New York: Washington Square Press, 1965).

Chapter Eleven
33 Watchman Nee, "Sit, Walk, Stand" (Bombay, India, Gospel Literature Service, 1957).
34 C.S. Lewis, *Mere Christianity* (Glasgow: Fount Paperbacks, 1977).
35 Doug Manning, "Don't take my grief away from me" (Oklahoma City, OK, In-sight Books, Inc., 1979).
36 Rick Warren, *The Purpose Driven Life* (Grand Rapids, MI: Zondervan, 2002).
37 A.W. Tozer, "The Pursuit of God" (Camp Hill, PA, Christian Publications, Inc.,1982).

Chapter Thirteen
38 Jeremy Camp, *There will be a day*, Speaking Louder Than Before, Brandon Ebel Company, 2008, compact disc.
39 Francis Collins, "The Language of God" (New York, Free Press, 2006).
40 Francis Collins, "The Language of God" (New York, Free Press, 2006).
41 http://www.quotationspage.com/quotes/Voltaire.
42 Addison Roads, *Hope Now*, All That Matters, Ino Records, 2008, compact disc.

LaVergne, TN USA
30 March 2011

222201LV00002B/127/P